Governance in the Digital Age

Governance in the Digital Age

A Guide for the Modern Corporate Board Director

BRIAN STAFFORD AND
DOTTIE SCHINDLINGER

WILEY

Library of Congress Cataloging-in-Publication Data:

ISBN 9781119546702 (Hardcover)
ISBN 9781119546733 (ePDF)
ISBN 9781119546740 (ePub)

Printed in the United States of America

V10008485_030119

We dedicate this book to diligent directors everywhere – your efforts to positively impact your organizations and our world inspire us to innovate.

Contents

Foreword

A book on the "digital director" is long overdue. It used to be that directors' technology skills were either not emphasized or not thought of as important, but now you can't ignore the issue. Now, the more literate each director (and by each director, I mean every single director) is on digitization, cybersecurity, data privacy, and technological innovation, the more effective the board ultimately is. Boards need to evolve from "bricks-and-mortar" and paper to digitization. This book – which charts an evolution that is just beginning – will be a welcome addition to the arena.

As several of the directors interviewed in this book point out, governance in the digital age is hard work. This is partly due to the lack of knowledge and experience that many directors – who tend to be men in their late 50s, 60s, or early 70s – have about the use of technology, including the definitions, the acronyms, and the application. These are things directors can learn on the job, but boards really need to diversify, namely by recruiting younger information technology-literate directors with diverse digital expertise. Those incoming younger directors won't necessarily have P&L experience—they will likely not have run major businesses like the other directors have—but they have a skillset that will be so important to the success of the board in the years ahead. Information technology is one of the top competency gaps that I see when I create competency matrices for boards, and it's also the number-one skill that boards are seeking in new directors. The competency needs to include things like

AI and blockchain – not just a passing familiarity with these areas, but someone who actually "lives it." A client said to me recently, "If we don't bring the proper IT expertise onto our board, we'll cease to exist within 10 years."

As the authors of this book point out in Chapter 2, these trends certainly impact recruitment, and are impacting the way directors communicate with one another, their usage of board portals, and their comfort with technology. There are still some obstacles being produced by older directors who insist on using pen and paper – they get left out of discussions on the board portal because they're not keeping up. There's a need for director education on technology literacy, as well as reinforcing usage of board portals and having a younger technology-literate director who can act as a catalyst to catapult the board and advise the senior management. It's incredibly important for directors to understand digitization, disruption, and the impact on business models that occurs as a result – and many boards are simply not up to speed. Directors need to be diversified – in age, skillset, understanding of technology, and gender – you need younger directors who understand the technology and the implications on business models. Or, as "next-gen" director Priya Cherian Huskins – who was interviewed for this book – put it, "It's worth noting that age is not always a good proxy for business acumen. There are important competencies, for example an understanding of social media and technology disruption, where next-gen leaders can shine."

Boards need to talk about term limits. If you're bringing a director on who is 42 years old, you don't want them to be there for 30 years. Boards should consider nine, twelve or fifteen-year term limits to encourage healthy diversity of age, gender, and skillsets on boards. The danger is that you can become "stale" very quickly – all it takes is a technological drift of about a year or two and you can find yourself being left behind.

Take, for example, the use of social media. Many companies now have social media policies for directors dictating how they should behave and modes of behavior around social media. But many directors tell me they just avoid social media because they don't know how to use it. One director asked me *last week,* "What's Twitter?" There needs to be education around tone, language, and usage – recruitment firms are now searching social media profiles of candidates to determine the level of risk and knowledge. If directors understand what each social media platform does, they will understand the rapid brand contagion that social media can produce for the company – which can be positive or negative. A few years ago, it used to be two to three days before an issue went public – now it's 10 minutes or less. If your brand can be brought into disrepute in a matter of minutes, directors have to be able to understand each platform, the risks social media could bring, and how to leverage it successfully. In response to social media, some boards are becoming more assertive – asking directors to disclose any incidents that could become common knowledge and cause harm. The use of Google Alerts is no longer adequate – you likely will need professional help to monitor issues being shared on social media and bring forward any issues for board discussion. For example, recently there was an issue where an executive grabbed a microphone and made disparaging comments to a female reporter – it was instantly on social media and caused adverse brand damage to the company within one hour. Directors have to do a lot of upfront prep work because once the crisis happens, it's too late to respond.

In Chapter 3, the authors explore some of the ways boards are dealing with new sources of risk presented by technology innovation and disruption. Many boards send all technology issues into a committee for discussion. Traditionally, the audit committee deals with all risk issues. But technology risk is different, and the audit committee may not necessarily be equipped to handle technology risk. I'm seeing more governance committees get recast as "governance and risk" committees to deal with a broader range of risk areas, including technology risk. Some boards are creating specific technology committees – which is not yet a widespread trend, but is becoming more common. If you consider that 90 percent of corporate assets are now digital/intangibles, technology has to be considered as part of material risk for the company. Boards need people on these committees who understand technology and can advise the company's CIO or CISO. The board should be able to lead, rather than follow, on technology issues. Younger directors who have that expertise can help companies see the future.

There is a great deal of new risk – including personal liability – because of technology. Lawyers are beginning to sue directors for their texting and cell phone interactions that occurred during board meeting times – attempting to demonstrate that directors have breached their duty of care by using technology inappropriately during meetings. There is a need for much greater rigor to demonstrate that you were paying attention, including the expectation that directors are using technology in a way that facilitates and enhances rather than distracts during board meetings. But technology can be a powerful tool, allowing boards, for example, to bring directors into the room who are in other jurisdictions – New York, London, Berlin, Sydney, Singapore, San Francisco, and so on. Technology is powerful, but it can become a powerful distraction – you have to make sure you have the best and brightest in the room who use tech wisely.

Chapter 6 provides some food for thought around directors and personal responsibility that ties in well to how boards can respond in the digital age. There is now a trend to have more individual areas of expertise among directors. It used to be that "we're all in this together" on boards, but as we begin to have individual competencies that are explicit on the board, each player brings different expertise to bear on discussions. Each one can review documents from their unique perspective and make recommendations at the board and committee level. It's no longer acceptable for any director to just sit back and be passive: you have to be more proactive in applying your unique expertise. I could envision a day in the future when we might have liability commensurate with director expertise – if there's a major hack and breach of privacy, lawyers and activists might begin to hold the board accountable for not having the right experts at the table. This puts pressure on boards to recruit based on competencies, similar to how the SEC changed its rules on financial competency on boards in the wake of the financial crisis in 2008.

Given the increased scrutiny and liability facing directors, many companies are investing in cyber-risk insurance. But, just as with any other type of insurance, having it doesn't mean you can be complacent – insurers look at your level of involvement and preparation and use that to determine paying damages. If you rely on insurance, it's already too late. It doesn't address the need for due diligence inside the boardroom. Insurance is a fail-safe – you still need to implement all the best practices that are outlined in this book.

Boards must adopt an attitude of resilience when it comes to technology innovation and disruption. It's a moving target, and if you don't keep up you're falling behind. Regular education sessions (every meeting) – bringing in experts to keep directors up to speed on technology, augmenting competencies, increasing budgets for education that are already generous, attending conferences – all of these things need to be part of every director's routine work. Boards are now retaining third-party technology experts – futurists, cyber-risk experts, inventors, others – to make sure the board is kept updated and has access to outside perspective to help validate what they hear from management. And, as the authors point out, boards are beginning to develop "personality profiles" that can either help or hinder their ability to adapt and build resilience.

I believe, as some directors have said to me, "We're in the middle of a revolution." We're at a tipping point with technology that is fundamentally changing how business works. Futurists are telling us how the world might look 10 to 20 years from now, and most industries will see radical transformation. Boards now have to emphasize how their businesses can remain nimble, plan ahead for how technology might disrupt their business models, anticipate where change will likely come from, grapple with "the unknown unknowns," and help management to be prepared.

The boards of the companies that are outperforming against their peers are aggressive about pushing information to management, rather than waiting for information from management. They have specific KPIs (key performance indicators) to tell the story of value creation, and they control the agenda. Technology is 40-60 percent of each agenda in these companies. But to do this you need directors who are confident in understanding technology. Many directors feel that they don't know what to do, and yet they are retained on boards because of their independence and not their level of competence. A good director has the credibility and gravitas to push down strategy and information to management – not micromanagement, but overseeing future change, digitization, and business models. Rubber-stamp boards – those that simply wait for instruction – are in denial. The board should never be in denial – there are no bad companies, only bad boards. This book will help directors know what's at stake and how they can adopt better practices to ensure the long-term health and viability of their enterprises.

Dr. Richard LeBlanc

Professor of Governance, Law & Ethics, York University, Faculty at the Directors College, and author of *The Handbook of Board Governance: A Comprehensive Guide for Public, Private and Not-for-Profit Board Members*, © 2016, John Wiley & Sons

Acknowledgments

This book was truly a team effort, involving hundreds of hours invested by multiple players to bring it across the goal line. We'd like to extend our deepest gratitude to all those who played a role in helping to develop this book. In particular, we extend our heartfelt gratitude to all those who shared their insights and expertise through the interviews we conducted, including Betsy Atkins, Jan Babiak, Leslie Campbell, Nelson Chan, Priya Cherian Huskins, Pamela Coles, Nora Denzel, Sue Forrester, John Hinshaw, Erin Lantz, Anastassia Lauterbach, Richard Leblanc, Ralph Loura, Colin Low, Merline Saintil, Margaret Whelan, and Laurie Yoler. Your wit and wisdom made this book special – thank you for generously sharing your stories.

We would also like to say a special thank you to Diligent team members Warren Allen, Zach Boisi, Amanda Carty, Meghan Day, Tania Dworjan, Amanda Finney, Maggie Fisher, Kerie Kerstetter, Annie Kors, Natalie Lazo, Elyse Maloni, Nick Price, and Leslie Tytka for their invaluable assistance – from providing input on the overall direction of the book, to assisting with director interviews, to reviewing and editing drafts, to assisting with research, copyediting, graphics, scheduling, and so much more. Additionally, we could not have completed this project if it were not for the team at Garfinkel and Associates, especially Steve Garfinkel, Jill Marquardt, and Samantha Rosen – your tireless efforts helped make this book a reality.

Finally, we want to thank all of our colleagues, family members, and friends for their unending and gracious support. In the pursuit of finishing this book, we had to turn down invitations and delay other obligations, and we thank you for your understanding and patience – we hope you enjoy reading the results.

About the Authors

Brian Stafford is Chief Executive Officer of Diligent Corporation, the leading provider of secure communication and collaboration services to board members and the C-Suite of leading organizations. Brian assumed the role of CEO in March 2015 and is responsible for all day-to-day operations with a primary focus on driving global growth by delighting its clients with great products.

Brian previously served as a partner at McKinsey & Company, where he founded and led their Growth Stage Tech Practice. While there, he concentrated on helping growth stage technology companies scale faster and did extensive work with software-as-a-service (SaaS) companies, focusing on sales operations and strategy, pricing, international growth, and team building. Prior to his tenure at McKinsey, Brian was the founder, president, and CEO of an automotive spinoff of Trilogy Software based in Austin, Texas.

Brian holds a Master's Degree in Computer Science from the University of Chicago and a Bachelor's in Science from the Wharton School at the University of Pennsylvania. He serves on the board of the Brooklyn Academy of Music (BAM).

Dottie Schindlinger is Vice President of Thought Leadership and Governance Technology Evangelist for Diligent Corporation. In her role, Dottie provides thought leadership on governance, cybersecurity, and technology topics through presentations to boards and executives dozens of times each year at events around the globe. Her work has been featured in *Forbes*, *The Wall Street Journal*, and in multiple governance and technology industry publications.

Dottie brings more than 20 years' experience in governance-related roles, including serving as a director, officer, committee chair, senior executive, board-support professional, governance consultant, and trainer for public, private, and nonprofit boards. She was a founding team member of the tech start-up BoardEffect – a board management software provider for nonprofit, education, and health-care boards, acquired by Diligent in late 2016. Dottie currently serves on the board of the Alice Paul Institute. She holds a Bachelor's of Arts in English from the University of Pennsylvania.

Introduction

What Does It Mean to Govern in the Digital Age?

Corporate governance has always been a challenging job, but there has likely never been a time when serving on a board has been more challenging and demanding than right now. Board oversight is charged with more risk than ever before, with directors having to confront a wide array of increasingly complex pressures from both inside and outside the company: an unpredictable geopolitical, environmental, economic, and social climate; workplace misconduct allegations against senior executives; public and regulatory outcry against companies that haven't adequately protected consumer data; activist shareholders working to replace or augment board directors with new and more diverse talent – the list goes on. Regardless of this complexity, directors are expected to be able to respond instantly to any situation that comes their way, with little tolerance from stakeholders for anything other than swift and positive outcomes. Directors are judged on their speed of action and their ability to accurately predict what is going to happen in an environment defined by unpredictability.

Meanwhile, the procedures and norms of board meetings have not changed since parliamentary procedure was codified in the late nineteenth century in *Robert's Rules of Order*, which encouraged careful deliberation of issues before making final decisions. Such a deliberate pace of decision making is not likely to be valued in an era best defined by Moore's Law, in which the speed of technological innovation and data processing nearly doubles every 18 months.[1] In this digital age, investors, shareholders, and other stakeholders expect instant results and have precious little patience for boards who take material time for careful consideration or reflection.

Perhaps this is one reason more directors are limiting the number of board appointments they now accept. In days past, serving on multiple boards was seen as a badge of honor and indicated a well-rounded board director. These days, proxy advisors warn companies about bringing on directors who are "overboarded." Even though directors might only meet a handful of times each year, they must accept responsibility for the overall success, or failure, of the enterprise.

With these mounting pressures, directors are seeking new processes and solutions to help make the board's complex job more manageable. Yet many current approaches fall short of transforming how boards govern.

One complicating factor is the modest pace of change in board diversity. Despite some positive recent changes in gender diversity,[2] corporate boards globally remain overwhelmingly male, older, and white – regardless of their companies' geographic region, industry, or customer demographics. Research shows that companies with gender-diverse boards outperform industry peers by several percentage points,[3] yet female directors occupy less than 17 percent of board seats globally, and at the present rate of increase corporate boards will not reach gender parity until 2048.[4] As concerning – if not more concerning in the digital age – is the lack of age diversity on corporate boards. Despite many efforts by companies to onboard younger directors, the average age of corporate board members continues to increase annually. Research shows that for companies on the S&P 500, 80 percent have directors aged 60 years or older; less than 5 percent of directors are aged 50 years or younger; and 21 percent of directors are aged 70 years or older.[5]

But the fact that the vast majority of board directors are not "digital natives" is only part of the problem. Recent research from Deloitte estimates that only 17 percent of S&P 500 company directors have technology expertise.[6] This lack of technology smarts in the boardroom can have real consequences. According to the same study, companies whose boards focus on recruiting directors with technology expertise are twice as likely to outperform the S&P 500 Index, by as much as 10 percent.

These issues raise the question: What approaches actually have the potential to help directors govern better in the digital age? In other words, what specific practices are companies using to help their directors gain the thoughtful insights needed to make complex decisions, while moving at the speed of a tweet? What should directors know about how governance practices are evolving in response to digital disruption and technological innovation? Most importantly, if directors find their boards are not keeping pace with digital-age demands, what practical solutions can they implement to gain advantage?

Purpose and Focus of This Book

In our work with more than 14,000 organizations and 500,000 directors and executives in more than 90 countries on all seven continents, we've seen a small but growing group of organizations begin to shift how they conceive of and enact the functions of governance. Traditional governance processes were developed in an era when the goal was *deliberation* – defined as "a long and careful consideration or discussion." Today, when nearly any question can be answered through a Google search or by speaking aloud to Amazon's "Alexa," many directors feel they should be able to have more direct access to the information needed to make strategic decisions. They are less inclined to wait for carefully curated reports containing data that is weeks old by the time they're distributed. Further, giving directors access to information only after it has been filtered multiple times by the management team presents real challenges to board oversight and accountability. Boards must – and are beginning to – ensure the *deliberative* process can keep pace with the digital age's speed of business. There's a lot at stake. Enterprises that leverage the speed of information and smarter technology to inform careful deliberation may quickly outpace their peers.[7]

Yet, most existing books on corporate governance focus on establishing core practices and principles designed to last throughout the tests of time. Only a handful of articles have been written on how governance practices are changing – and most of these articles report the actions of a single board. This book is an attempt to begin filling what we perceive to be a gap in corporate governance literature and to provide directors with a handy summary of innovative practices as boards around the globe grapple with the challenges of governing in the digital age. Through interviews with global corporate directors and senior executives, and by researching the latest books, trade publications, and news sources, we have compiled dozens of examples of changes to corporate boardroom practices. Additionally, we've attempted to document some of our own observations on changes in corporate governance – drawing from interactions with thousands of board members and senior executives for whom we develop and deliver governance software.

That said, we absolutely do not believe that this book is definitive – far from it. Rather, we hope that this brief book will inspire others to join the conversation on how board directors can govern successfully in an era marked by rapid digital transformation and disruption.

What's in This Book and How to Use It

Over the past 15 years – partly in reaction to new governance challenges – organizations have begun to implement innovative governance practices with the power to profoundly improve how their board functions, enhance director engagement, and lead to greater results.

As pressure mounts for directors to quickly arrive at definitive answers, new tools are under development to allow companies and directors to reconsider when, what, and how often the board receives critical information. With some, companies will be able to provide directors more direct access to data, fueling better queries and data-driven decisions. Yet even with technology delivering answers faster than humans, it will still be up to directors to ask the right questions. In this governance evolution, the role of a director may shift from that of "trusted advisor," to that of "questioner-in-chief" – the individual who brings keen insight derived from experience, and who is able to craft questions that catapult the organization to new levels of performance.

Given the increasing complexity of governance work, the time is right for companies to look beyond tools focused only on building efficiency in obsolete processes and to gain advantage through technologies that enhance leadership performance.

The process of governing is in the midst of a major transition. However, this transition has received too little attention, and directors have gleaned only a small handful of practical strategies, examples, or guidance. As a result, directors – from those who have been in the role for a day to those who have served for decades – are hungry for insights, especially from peers who have faced similar challenges.

Whether you are a director, CEO, general counsel, company secretary, or other individual involved in governance work, this book is for you. Here you will find a collection of insights, examples, templates, and strategies designed to help directors, senior executives, and governance professionals survive (and thrive) while governing in the digital age – all kept brief so you can finish reading it in a short period of time.

This book is far less about specific governance technologies, and more about how directors and boards are evolving, in large part as a reaction to technological innovation and new pressures. In Part 1, we share insights from the interviews we conducted with directors of major public companies from around the globe on specific governance practices in the digital age. The directors we interviewed generously shared their stories in the hopes that others might benefit from their experiences. Throughout the book, you will find practical guidance, wisdom, and insights from current directors on successfully navigating governance in the digital age. As we were not able to include every interview in its entirety in the book, you'll find additional interviews, downloadable samples, and other resources on the book's companion website, located at https://diligent.com/governance-in-the-digital-age.

This book has also attempted to synthesize the latest research, collected from a broad array of sources, on how governance is changing in response to digital pressures. Whenever possible, we included practical strategies that we believe to be suggested by governance research, with the goal of making that research more practical for directors, executives, and others involved in governance work.

In Part 2, we've synthesized the key findings from our interviews and research into a framework we're calling Board Behavioral Profiles. Similar to psychological behavioral profiles, which describe the characteristics, traits, and behavior patterns of individuals, our suggested Board Behavioral Profiles reflect the common traits, boardroom behaviors, and other factors we found being described again and again in our interviews. In Chapter 7, we describe the most commonly reported factors by arranging them into four profiles, including the Foundational Board, the Structural Board, the Catalyst Board, and the Futuristic Board. These identify and group together the unique approaches boards are taking to navigate the challenges of the digital age.

Despite the old adage, "If you know one board, you know *one board*," directors told us they felt these four profiles resonated with their own experiences – and could potentially help others chart their own paths. While it would be wrong to expect that the Board Behavioral Profiles will perfectly match the experiences of every director, those who were interviewed for this book hoped that by sharing their stories and insights, other directors might gain clarity on the best way to navigate digital realities and adapt board governance practices. Our hope is that this framework gives directors a handy cheat sheet to use in conversations with fellow directors to describe their experiences governing in the digital age and, should the board feel a change is warranted, a primer on how to make the desired changes.

In Chapter 8, we bring together the governance practices described in Part 1 with the Board Behavioral Profiles developed in Part 2 – exploring how boards of different profiles might approach best practices in the digital age. As this new roadmap is being charted in a rapidly evolving landscape, it's reasonable to assume governance strategies will similarly need to evolve over time. On the companion website – https://diligent.com/governance-in-the-digital-age – we invite you to share your own insights, especially if you have feedback to share based on your own experiences governing in the digital age.

Notes

1. Staff, Investopedia, "Moore's Law," *Investopedia*, Investopedia, 8 Aug. 2018, https://www.investopedia.com/terms/m/mooreslaw.asp.
2. According to the 2017 Spencer Stuart U.S. Corporate Board Index, 80 percent of corporate boards now include two or more female directors, although women occupy only 22 percent of the board seats in S&P 500 companies. See "A World of Insight," Spencer Stuart, https://www.spencerstuart.com/research-and-insight/ssbi-2017-board-composition-part-3esearch-and-insight/ssbi-2017-board-composition-part-3.
3. Data from "The Tipping Point – Women on Boards and Financial Performance," MSCI, https://www.msci.com/www/research-paper/the-tipping-point-women-on/0538947986, which reviewed the performance of

U.S. companies during a five-year period from 2011 to 2016, found that those that began the period with at least three female board directors had 10 percentage point gains in return on equity (ROE), and 37 percent gains in earnings per share (EPS). This is compared to companies with no female directors experiencing a 1 percentage point loss in ROE and –8 percent in EPS over the same time period.

4. Equilar Blog, "Equilar | Pay for Performance Disconnect Cited as Main Shareholder Concern in Say on Pay Vote Failures," https://www.equilar.com/blogs/212-boards-will-reach-gender-parity-in-2055.html.

5. Sources: KPMG, home.kpmg.com/jm/en/home/insights/2017/03/age-diversity-within-boards-of-directors-of-the-s-p-500-companie.html; and PricewaterhouseCoopers, "Board Composition: Consider the Value of Younger Directors on Your Board," PwC, https://www.pwc.com/YoungerDirectors.

6. "Bridging the Boardroom's Technology Gap," Deloitte United States, https://www2.deloitte.com/insights/us/en/focus/cio-insider-business-insights/bridging-boardroom-technology-gap.html. The report shows that 31.3 percent of the companies whose boards have focused on recruiting directors with technology expertise have outperformed the S&P 500 Index by 10 percent over the past three years.

7. Andy Kiersz, "Here's How Much You Would Have Made Investing $1,000 in Facebook, Amazon, Netflix and 19 Other Major Companies Back in the Day," *Business Insider*, 15 July 2018, https://www.businessinsider.com/facebook-amazon-walmart-stock-prices-investment-performance-2018-7#a-1000-investment-in-facebook-after-its-may-18-2012-ipo-would-be-worth-over-5000-as-of-july-3-2018-1.

PART 1

Governance Practices in the Digital Age

CHAPTER 1

Ensuring Value Creation (Despite Volatility)

Most companies have growth periods and value periods. You grow and then you harvest.[1]

– Margaret Whelan, Corporate Director of TopBuild and Mattamy Homes

What is value creation in the digital age? It's a home-building company actively reallocating its capital to the markets with the most need and the least competition. It's a medical IT company[2] developing products that respond to pain points in customers' daily workflows. It's a mail-order provider of DVDs adjusting to changing consumer behavior to become a world leader in scripted programming.

Value creation is different from growth. Growth is about short-term returns and capital expansion, with less focus on longer-term consequences. Value creation, by contrast, is a long-term strategy that takes into account how companies invest in innovation and sustainability.

Importantly for corporate boards of directors, value creation today goes beyond immediate decisions on dividends and investment strategies to maintaining a durable and sustainable business model. Think of it as building a strong company as well as a strong stock – a dual mission that's more challenging than ever in today's global landscape of technological complexity. And think about it as staying ahead of risks and opportunities. At any moment, a new innovation like blockchain or artificial intelligence, or virtual reality can irrevocably upend business as usual, even for the most entrenched global leader.

Stakeholders agree that boards need to play a more involved role in making their corporations valuable to customers, investors, and the overall marketplace. BlackRock, State Street Global Advisors, Vanguard, and others have been pressing for governance practices that support long-term, sustainable value creation.[3] Evolutions in these practices have included mandatory sustainability reports for publicly traded companies in Singapore and proxy statements in the United States that have evolved from check-the-box compliance statements to rich windows into a company's strategy, performance, compensation, and culture.[4]

Board members already make pivotal decisions on acquisitions, investments, marketplace expansions, executive hires, and more. But in an environment of constant and often cataclysmic change, they must replace the caretaker model through which they traditionally view such decisions with what consulting firm Bain describes as a "private equity" approach.[5] They must look at decisions with the sharp, opportunity-focused eye of an investor, as well as the caution of a steward.

The right board leadership can steer a $500 million company into becoming a $10 billion leader, while ineffectual guidance holds a similar power in the opposite direction. Or, to paraphrase the famous words attributed to Intel's Andy Grove, only the value creators survive.

How can a forward-thinking board make the shift from cautious steward to innovation catalyst? Even the most time-efficient director possesses only 24 hours in each day. And board processes, steeped in decades of tradition, may not be agile enough to respond to the heady demands of value creation.

We believe quick wins in this complex area can be achieved. First, focus on operational engagement, specifically implementing fresh tactics for collaboration, shaping board structures (especially committees) for the value creation mission, and using technology to stay in touch with what's going on inside and outside of the organization. Then examine your Board Behavioral Profile. Which traits does your board currently exhibit? Consider how your profile might need to shift for greater value creation.

Embrace New Ways of Working Together

Becoming a value-focused board doesn't happen instantly, with one epiphany at an alpine board retreat. It happens over time, with incremental changes to business as usual. In a November/December 2017 *Harvard Business Review* article about the "new innovation imperative," former Mastercard CEO Robert Selander emphasized that big ideas typically don't spark transformative change.[6] It usually takes several ongoing discussions about several ideas, good and bad.

Cambia Health Solutions CEO Mark Ganz put this premise to work by turning its PowerPoint–driven board meetings to open discussions.[7] Through encouraging thought-provoking questions, his board improved their partnership with management and increased the value delivered by individual members.

Boards are recognizing the need to solicit new and different viewpoints in order to stay relevant. Board diversity is key to board resilience, an area that will be explored further in the next chapter. Specific to value creation, many directors and other governance professionals are finding that bringing in a broader range of perspectives can keep a board more closely in touch with change and better equipped to talk about it. Onboarding new directors can also change board dynamics for richer, deeper conversations and faster, sharper decision making.

"They say that if you have at least two or three women on a board, it really changes the way a board processes things. The same study has been done with digital directors," said Betsy Atkins, CEO and founder of Baja Corporation, who serves as a director on the boards of directors of Cognizant, Wynn Resorts, SL Green Realty, Schneider Electric, and Volvo Cars. "You need, at minimum, two digitally savvy directors to understand the rate of change, technology, and how to use technology to bring costs down, take friction and steps out of the customer journey, and truly understand future differentiated business models."[8]

How important are these broad-ranging perspectives? Allstate CEO Tom Wilson cited valuable insights into customer behavior from a board member experienced in "connected car" startups and the manufacturing/OEM space.[9] And imagine the fate of Netflix if someone hadn't flagged changing habits in TV and movie consumption as a game-changing trend.

According to Ralph Loura, who's been an executive with Rodan + Fields, Clorox, and HP, boards can change their value-creation outcomes by becoming more digitally focused. "Like a lot of things that have happened around IT in the past, supply chain automation, financial consolidation, this was at first thought of as 'Oh, this is just an IT project.' But then something like 70 percent of all CRM implementations were considered failing at some level, and people realized they were treating these implementations like an IT project, instead of business projects."[10]

Disruption in the Entertainment Industry Inspires a "Fashionable" Startup

Sometimes the best way to sense that a business model is changing is to see it in action. StitchFix founder and CEO Katrina Lake was studying Blockbuster and Netflix in her previous role as a venture capitalist when she realized the way people were consuming movies was evolving toward a subscription model.[11] She sensed that similar changes might be happening in retail and built a $977 million company on that insight.

Bringing on members with fresh perspectives on value creation is only part of the battle, however. Boards must be able to draw out their insights and maximize their contributions.

Education, engagement, and encouragement are places to start. Nelson Chan, who serves as Chairman of the Board of Adesto Technologies and is a corporate director of Deckers Outdoor Corp., believes that

"We carve out the time to ask these big questions. It's as important – more important – than dealing with audit or comp."[12]

For example, "We might carve out a half day to work with an expert or go outside and see what's happening on the bleeding age of tech for transforming the marketplace. We visited companies that do that like Google or investment firms focusing on tech startups, and we asked them to show us what they are up to as a way to educate the board."

Checklist for Cultivating and Maintaining Value-Focused Collaboration

Making new methods of collaboration stick can be a challenging proposition – especially for a time-strapped board with entrenched ways of working together. Here are a few suggestions for getting started:

- Foster a boardroom culture of respectful disagreement, curiosity, candor, and open debate. Make the boardroom a space where constructive criticism is welcomed by directors and senior managers alike as an important ingredient in growth.
- Expose board members to new ideas. This could be through meeting with experts from different and/or related industries and reading broadly on current issues.
- Get the board out of the boardroom periodically. Visit your company's primary operations, research and development (R&D) department, and other key divisions. Meet with key customers and investors to ensure relevance.
- Expand the diversity of backgrounds, skillsets, and leadership styles represented in the boardroom. More unique perspectives can lead to better outcomes.
- Remember that trust is an essential component to a collaborative mind-set. People share more ideas, with greater candor, when they don't fear condemnation for their contributions.

Take Value Creation to Committee(s)

Value creation is too important – and the circumstances driving it too volatile – to address only six to nine times a year. Many boards enlist their audit or risk committee to conduct research on investment, risk, and industry trends and actively participate in strategic planning. Ideally, committees will be monitoring and evaluating progress toward the company's strategic goals and regularly updating the full board on progress.

In this past decade of digital transformation, some boards are upping the ante by making structural adjustments specifically for innovation – a key component of (and some might say synonym for) value creation. In 2012, French tire manufacturer Michelin established an "innovation governance system" led by a Corporate Innovation Board.[13] Members include product line managers, the corporate development manager, an external member, and the manager for research, development, and innovation. This board's mission is to define innovation strategy, ensure a dynamic innovation ecosystem (which includes customer and market feedback), and to make decisions in areas such as innovation investment and research direction.

At Rolls-Royce, a company that Pamela Coles, Company Secretary, praises for its focus on innovation, the board pairs up directors with different backgrounds for site visits. "They'll see things differently," she said. "They'll ask different questions."[14]

But just establishing a special committee or initiative for value creation is not enough. Such a committee needs to make an impact on value creation and be recognized by stakeholders for its role in doing so.

A recent situation with Procter & Gamble provided an interesting and powerful example.[15] P&G has an Innovation and Technology Committee tasked to oversee the acquisition, implementation, and tracking of technical and commercial innovation. Yet in early 2018, activist investor Nelson Peltz, who oversees roughly $3 billion in P&G stock, joined the board positing that P&G hasn't created an important brand in two decades. He referred to corporate R&D as "a hobby" and has called for cuts.

Companies, including their boards, need to champion technological innovation and make it an overarching priority. Laurie Yoler, who was a founding member of Tesla's board of directors, and now serves on the boards of Church & Dwight, Zoox, Bose Corporation, and Noon Home, explains, "The issues a company faces, like cyber, are so broad in their impact that you need to determine what the full board should review vs. what the tech committee should handle. How will the full board get comfortable with tech terms and issues if they are relegated to a single committee?"[16]

A Global Take on Board Tech Literacy[17]

Anastassia Lauterbach, PhD, a technology strategist, is founder and CEO of 1AU-Ventures Ltd. She serves as a director on the boards of directors of Dun & Bradstreet, Wirecard, and Censhare, and she serves as a senior advisor to McKinsey and Company. Dr. Lauterbach is also the author of a new book, *The Artificial Intelligence Imperative: A Practical Roadmap for Business.*

What level of tech literacy do you see in your work with boards?

Even though IT is one of the top drivers of competitiveness today, IT is a new field for most directors, especially in Europe. On German boards, for example, even cyber-security is considered to be a novelty. Most directors did not study computer science or technology. There are soft factors at work, too. Many directors don't want to admit that they lack IT understanding or struggle to dedicate time to self-study. Technologists often aren't helpful either. They speak in jargon, use a lot of abbreviations, and don't translate their visions for "normal executives."

Why don't boards recruit directors with more IT knowledge?

Because of fit issues. If CISOs (Chief Information Security Officers) and risk managers go through the interview process and speak candidly with leadership, you might hear, "This is a great opportunity but not a great cultural fit."

Furthermore, most of my peers working in technology are not used to the culture in the boardroom, which is overwhelmingly white, male, and "gray." In my experience speaking with board members who are age 65-plus, these directors are very interested in what you have to say and are amazed at what's happening in technology, but then they don't move forward because of that cultural fit. There might be a bit of an unconscious bias. People love the familiar. We love having people who are just like us in our companies. But boards need to recruit people who think differently or have a different area of expertise and need to give them encouragement. Often it comes down to the chairman's ability to establish a culture of respect and curiosity.

This comfort level builds with time and familiarity. When I was the only technologist on the board and I would ask questions of the CIO, all the other directors would check out. Now that there is a second technologist on our board, there's more engagement. The directors are more

(continued)

active in asking questions. Technology matters can't be outsourced just to directors with strong IT backgrounds. Everyone should be involved.

What specific board practices have you seen change because of the rapidly increasing speed of information?

Directors are spending more time with technology teams. They're facilitating exchanges with other companies within their networks, and they want to see technical people at every strategic and operational discussion. Directors are sharing information from conferences and what they're reading.

Governance is more or less a historical concept, and our current frameworks are backwards-looking in a time when we need them to be more forward-thinking. Boards need to know what they don't know, which requires a lot of courage. Directors need to be able to ask questions and be honest about what they don't understand, or they won't be able to provide the level of oversight and insight required today.

Track the Right Metrics and Trends

How can directors keep tabs of external market trends and how their corporations need to react to create and maintain value?

A perfect solution might look a little like the classic television show *Star Trek*. Directors would be able to create a "Vulcan mind meld" with every important internal and external stakeholder – think department heads, heads of startups and key competitors, pivotal activists, and investors – importing the latest intel on R&D, risk, market opportunity, and more into their brains. They would use the logic of Mr. Spock to distill the salient points into an actionable view of the technological, commercial, and financial landscape. And like Captain Kirk, they would be able to dive headfirst into the unknown because they trusted their crew to come up with creative and innovative solutions to any obstacles they might encounter.

Until such sci-fi capabilities become reality, however, boards will have to make do with available tools and processes. This includes meetings and events with customers and shareholders and IT applications like dashboards, which are emerging and evolving in sophistication with today's overall wave of digital transformation.

One straightforward way to find out what's going on with employees and customers: get out of the boardroom and interact with them. When Chip Bergh began as Levi's CEO and joined the company's board, one of the first things he did to investigate its falling sales was embark on a month-long "listening tour" to meet with 60 top executives.[18] In his second month on the job, his in-depth interview with a customer in Bangalore yielded a new tagline: "Live in Levi's."

Corporate director Laurie Yoler spoke of her own experiences as a board member. "We just did a tour of our R&D center to learn how the company handles innovation and development and the full board received such value from the visit."[19]

But the speed of digital transformation inherently presents challenges to boards striving to stay educated, she added. "The tech consultants that come into the boardroom tend to be one-off speakers, which isn't the same level of engagement and longevity that you have with your auditors, outside counsel, or compensation consultants. For example, if you're in a manufacturing firm, you might focus on specific robotic systems, but those might only be the most important 'right now' and change in six months."

When such "feet on the ground" approaches are impractical, a digital dashboard can give board members a reading of the landscape. Innovations in data collection and analytics have made an unprecedented amount of data available for decision making, increasingly with real-time availability. The trick, with dashboards and with overall governance, is in keeping board members out of the weeds.

How involved should a board be in company operations? What should the members know – when and at what level of detail? At what point does informed oversight cross the line into information overload and micromanaging? The answers will vary across companies and evolve with the digital age. Based on our conversations with directors across industries and around the world, we believe boards can start by:

- **Keeping abreast of macro trends**, which today might include blockchain, virtual reality, augmented reality, artificial intelligence, and robotics.

- **Narrowing your focus to what really matters.** Out of all the thousands of trends you could be tracking in the external environment, identify the ones that are most relevant to your organization. Track the metrics that most accurately reflect the performance and health of each department. Then synthesize this into potential opportunities (or risks) to corporate value.

- **Asking provocative questions**, like does your current reporting structure enable success? Are tech budgets reflecting strategic priorities? How does your brand and business model compare with peers (including new entrants)? Does either need a refresh to be more contemporary?

- **Measuring success** with quantitative measurements and analysis and making sure management rewards, incentives, and promotions push innovation, rather than take the safer road.

- **Leading by example,** with directors who embrace tech trends, actively integrate them into strategy, and clearly communicate investment decisions.

Certain areas will always feed into value creation, no matter what your geographic region, industry focus, or company size. These include risk management, corporate citizenship, and the ability to inform strategy with perfectly timed insights. These areas will be discussed in greater detail later in this chapter. Up next, however, we'll discuss one of the most important components of successful value creation: the people you put on your board and the structures and processes you give them to do their best work.

Key Takeaways on Value Creation

- **Change up board dynamics.** Board diversity is key to both value creation and resilience. Bringing in new perspectives leads to richer, deeper conversations and sharper decision making.

- **Expand board education outside the boardroom.** Visit other companies, work with experts, and encourage fellow board members to ask big questions.

- **Get comfortable with technology.** Relegating tech to a single committee leaves much of the board out of decisions that could have a broad impact on the company.

- **Don't forget employees and customers.** Learn how your corporation needs to react to create and maintain value by interacting with employees and customers.

- **Examine your Board Behavioral Profile.** What are the traits of your board profile and how might it need to shift for greater value creation? (See Chapter 7 for more details.)

Building Value through the Right Practices and People[20]

Margaret Whelan is a real estate industry executive and founder and CEO of Whelan Advisory. She also serves on the boards of directors of TopBuild, Mattamy Homes, John Burns Real Estate Consulting, and the Housing Innovation Alliance, along with four other nonprofit boards.

What overall practices are having the biggest impact in terms of financial success?

It's important to set the right tone and standards from the top, establish a growth plan through the CEO, have a board that is engaged and continuously refreshed to bring new energy and ideas into the room, and create an innovation strategy to think about things outside the box. The board's primary role, in my view, is to help the CEO to anticipate what's around the corner. That's easier said than done these days, as digitization is accelerating the rate of change and adoption rates for new products and services.

Another positive trend is quality over quantity. There is a link between board size and action. Look at the size of the Wells Fargo or GE boards and what happened in those companies. There were many smart people, but with GE there was atrophy in the business model, and at Wells Fargo the culture facilitated some poor judgment. Ultimately, having a large number of directors didn't help the shareholders.

For the right people, should you look for former CEOs or for board members with other skillsets, like next-gen directors with digital experience?

When you look at putting in next-generation directors, it reminds me of five years ago when I was looking to join my first corporate board. The message was, "We need a woman on the board. We're not looking at your resume, your skills, your capabilities, or your achievement. We just need a woman." I avoided those positions. More recently the focus has been on attracting younger directors because they can bring such a diverse and valuable perspective.

Today boards are saying, "We need someone who's a little younger, they have so much value to add as they work, live, and communicate in different and often more efficient ways." I'm a Gen Xer, working with a lot of Baby Boomers, wondering what the Millennials are thinking. Why not give them a seat at the table? In a lot of cases, their fresh perspective, even if they have yet to achieve their full professional potential, can still bring a lot of value add to a room that's populated with aging Boomers that aren't always fully engaged. PwC just published results of their director survey, and for the second year in a row half of the participants believe that at least one of their fellow board members is not adding any value. A young person with a fresh perspective is a big improvement versus someone who's disengaged. Maybe we need to think about board composition differently and be open to busy younger directors joining for a term or two, versus retired executives who stay too long.

On the other side, if everyone in the boardroom is putting on their superhero capes because they've all been CEOs, CFOs, or had other senior executive roles, they are often used to having all the opinions, all the influence. They're not always used to voting, and they can have strong personalities or opinions that less assertive directors can hide behind. Those directors don't speak up or challenge others because they're afraid they'll be replaced. When a board runs well, each person has a seat at the table, an even vote, and an informed opinion to share.

(continued)

How are you seeing companies become more diverse?

I'm in housing and construction, which is a very male-dominated industry. I work with a female CEO who is also chairman of a publicly traded housing company; more than half of her direct reports are female. That board recently announced two new female directors, so they now have a majority female board in an industry where half the boards don't even have one woman director. How was she able to find talented female directors when other companies are saying that they can't find any qualified female candidates? She brought in two very different candidates, including one with a retail background.

Notes

1. Excerpt from telephone interview with Margaret Whelan, 24 July 2018.
2. "Expert Solutions: The Future of Digital Value Creation," *Homepage*, https://wolterskluwer.com/company/newsroom/news/2018/02/expert-solutions-the-future-of-digital-value-creation.html.
3. Holly J. Gregory, "Governing Through Disruption: A Boardroom Guide for 2018." *Practical Law*, Thomson Reuters, 2017, https://www.sidley.com/-/media/publications/novdec17_govcounselor.pdf.
4. "The Proxy Statement: 4 Best Practices for the 2018 Season," *Boardroom Resources*, https://boardroomresources.com/insight/the-proxy-statement-4-best-practices-for-the-2018-season/.
5. "Portfolio Value Creation," Bain Brief – Bain & Company, https://www.bain.com/consulting-services/private-equity/portfolio-value-creation.aspx.
6. Linda A. Hill and George Davis, "Boards: Innovation Is Your Responsibility Too," *Harvard Business Review*,

24 November-December 2017, https://hbr.org/2017/11/the-boards-new-innovation-imperative.

7. Ibid.

8. Excerpts from telephone interview with Betsy Atkins, 21 Aug. 2018.

9. Tomas Pereira, "How Board Skills Vary by Director Age Groups," *Grading Global Boards of Directors on Cybersecurity*, https://corpgov.law.harvard.edu/2018/04/04/how-board-skills-vary-by-director-age-groups/.

10. Excerpts from telephone interview with Ralph Loura, 23 July 2018.

11. Katrina Lake, "Stitch Fix's CEO on Selling Personal Style to the Mass Market," *Harvard Business Review*, May–June 2018, pp. 36–40.

12. Excerpt from telephone interview with Nelson Chan, 3 Aug. 2018.

13. "Comité Groupe de L'Innovation: Le Corporate Innovation Board Michelin," *Pneus MICHELIN : plus De 200 Matériaux Pour Une Performance Totale | Michelin*, https://www.michelin.com/eng/innovation/innovation-strategy/organization-and-governance.

14. Excerpt from telephone interview with Pamela Coles, 7 Aug. 2018.

15. Barrett J. Brunsman, "P&G Activist Investor Nelson Peltz to Sit on Key Board Committees," Bizjournals.com, *The Business Journals*, 21 Feb. 2018, https://www.bizjournals.com/cincinnati/news/2018/02/21/p-g-activist-investor-nelson-peltz-to-sit-on-key.html.

16. Excerpt from telephone interview with Laurie Yoler, 2 Aug. 2018.

17. Excerpts from telephone interview with Anastassia Lauterbach, PhD, 15 Aug. 2018.

18. Chip Bergh, "The CEO of Levi Strauss on Leading an Iconic Brand Back to Growth," *Harvard Business Review*, July–August 2018, pp. 34–39.

19. Excerpt from telephone interview with Laurie Yoler, 2 Aug. 2018.

20. Excerpt from telephone interview with Margaret Whelan, 24 July 2018.

CHAPTER 2

Building a Resilient Board

Your most important duty to shareholders is to make sure that the enterprise thrives. To do that, the board has to be resilient – not only keep up with the rate of change but help management "look around the corners" to anticipate risks and competitive marketplace dynamics.[1]

– Betsy Atkins

In today's world, it's difficult to ensure that nothing ever goes wrong – because change will happen, and quickly, so adaptability is crucial. Consider the digital, market, and regulatory disruptions seen in just the twenty-first century so far:

- Business-to-consumer models shifting from bricks-and-mortar to e-commerce
- The emergence of social media networks, with implications for consumer marketing, sales models, and reputation management

- The impact of big data
- Increased pressure on companies to consider environmental and social impact
- New generations of consumers with different values, preferences, and buying habits

Change, and the resulting corporate churn, are not new phenomena, according to corporate director Margaret Whelan. "If you look back at the 1960s, companies in the S&P 500 had an average tenure of 33 years on the list. These days, nearly half the current S&P 500 is forecast to be replaced within the next 10 years. Either they go bankrupt, get acquired, or struggle and shrink, mostly because of a failure to embrace technological disruption. Unfortunately, Sears is another good example of this phenomenon."[2]

Yet today more than ever, disruption is transforming "business as usual" for boards. "The rapid pace of change and the breadth of the topics make [digital disruption] a particularly challenging area for board members to stay up-to-speed," said corporate director Laurie Yoler.[3]

As directors assume their broader role in an accelerating world, how can they make their own operations – and the corporations they serve – more resilient? By thinking like a communications network and looking at their infrastructure, performance, and composition. (See Figure 2.1.)

Resilience through Board Infrastructure

Having operated in an environment of corporate volatility for over a decade, today's boards are recognizing the need to adjust their usual ways of doing things.

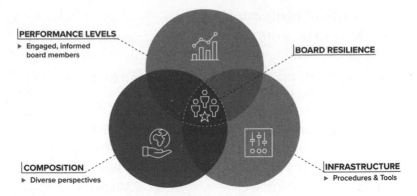

Figure 2.1 Resilient boards consider their infrastructure, performance, and composition.

For example, five-year plans, which may be obsolete in 18 months, are shifting to a more agile approach to decision making. According to corporate director Betsy Atkins, It's all about keeping up with the velocity of change by bringing on diverse directors and training directors to actually look for market dynamics, because even a successful business like GE can suddenly find they've become irrelevant. You can't sit back on your laurels at all. Directors have to look at their companies and ask: "Are we about to become Blockbuster Video or Borders Books because we're dismissing new business models?"[4]

But survival in the business world today isn't just about ongoing proactive planning. It's also about reacting to sudden change, including crises. Do boards right now have structures and processes in place for spotting risks before they become disasters? Many factors outside of the boardroom have led to crises like the fake accounts and fraud at Wells Fargo and sweeping breach of customer information at Equifax. But each organization's crisis happened on the board's watch. In many cases, processes were lacking for identifying contributing factors at the board level (for example, conflicts of interest and poor oversight) and for taking action.

Weaknesses in both of these aspects of value creation can be addressed through strengthening governance culture, structures, and processes. A stronger culture involves fostering respectful inquiry, encouraging (and graciously accepting) constructive criticism, thinking critically, and seeking diverse opinions. It also may involve adopting a "Growth Mindset," as coined by psychologist Carol Dweck, which emphasizes lifelong learning and embracing failures as opportunities for growth.

In terms of structure, boards can separate the chair and CEO roles to avoid potential conflicts of interest, monitor and enforce the independence of their directors, foster board diversity, and strengthen the role of committees.

For processes, director evaluations can be one powerful tool for building board resilience. "As we're seeing performance management tools for employees become more frequent, rather than just once a year, maybe the same thing could happen with board performance feedback," said Yoler.[5]

It's tempting for a time-strapped board to see self-evaluations as a "check the box" activity. Yet as business risks and economic volatility continue to increase, poor board performance can put a company, its investors, and others at risk. Furthermore, according to advisory and executive search firm Russell Reynolds, activist investors are expected to increase their scrutiny of director performance as they continue to influence board decision making, process, and composition.[6]

Every organization with a board should be conducting annual evaluations, whether they're required to or not. What's more, boards could welcome the evaluation process as a springboard for insights, action, corporate performance, and growth. Regular assessments enable a board to take stock of the areas that require attention – like best practices for handling sensitive customer data – and create board development plans accordingly.

What should directors and other governance professionals keep in mind when developing assessment criteria and using matrices, evaluations, and other tools to build board resilience?

Measure the Right Things

The board evaluation process needs to get at the heart of effective performance. Some criteria related to effective performance might include:

- Preparedness (or lack thereof)
- Expertise
- Ability to accurately assess concerns related to local, federal, and international law
- Knowledge of, and adherence to, current cybersecurity practices, which is vital in today's age of phishing, malware, and other cyber threats
- When developing your evaluation criteria and questions, be sufficiently comprehensive. Many organizations use only a single questionnaire to rate their board's performance. The results of these assessments tend to skew high and provide limited visibility into individual director performance. Additionally, online resources have become available for strengthening facilitation, refining formats, and putting board evaluation results into action.[7]

Use Online Tools for Greater Insights and Candor

When board evaluations are distributed and collected manually or by email, with corporate secretaries chasing down board members to complete their forms, it's not only a time- and labor-intensive process, anonymity is inherently compromised. An automated evaluation process, such as can be conducted through a secure online portal, presents several advantages. Not only does information flow more swiftly and easily to multiple locations and parties, the anonymous nature of this evaluation method increases a board's chances of getting unfiltered, honest remarks. Such forthcoming information could allow boards to spot risks and address sensitive issues earlier, before they become crises.

In addition, online forms (if they're customizable) give governance professionals more bandwidth to ask different kinds of questions and focus on the director performance criteria pertinent to their situation, from "comes prepared to meetings" to "provides useful insights" to "brings important expertise and a high level of competence."

What's more, with digital evaluation tools, you're collecting data across multiple competency areas and over time in a digital format that lends itself well to future analysis. Pair digital board evaluations with data analytics, and your board has a powerful dashboard for spotting vulnerabilities, identifying trends, and boosting performance.

Encourage Directors to Continuously Self-Educate and Improve

When asked who's responsible for board resilience – the individual director or the board as a whole – corporate director Betsy Atkins emphasized the importance of proactive learning on the part of the director, particularly in the area of self-education. "You listen to earnings calls from your competitors, not just your company. You read analyst reports and seek out industry reports from Forrester, Gartner, McKinsey, Accenture, and Bain. You should also be looking at the information that comes from futurists like Mary Meeker and events like the Global Innovation Summit + Week and resources like MIT.

"You ought to be keeping an eye on the macro trends happening both in and beyond your own industry, because they're going to affect your business," she added. "Ten years ago, the macro trend was mobility, and now everybody designs things to be mobile first. So, what are the macro trends today? Artificial intelligence and machine learning. There are also new business models like marketplaces and macro trends like the gig economy."[8]

In short: "Directors can't be passive receptacles of what their companies share. They need to build their own informed frameworks. And if they're going to be personally accountable, they need to stay contemporary."

Resilience through Board Performance

Communications networks can't afford to have some branches experiencing weak signals and disruption and others dropping off entirely. Similarly, organizations can't afford to let the performance of their directors falter in today's era of change and volatility.

In the words of Merline Saintil, who serves on the boards of Banner Corporation and Nav, Inc., "We are in the midst of an accelerating and daunting pace of change."[9]

Especially in this environment, she explained. "It's important to be open to different perspectives and understand that you don't have to agree all the time. I find that what's most beneficial about the two corporate boards that I'm on is that people really challenge each other. You come out of some meetings feeling exhausted because you have been completely immersed in thought-provoking ideas for hours, but that's the way it should be."

Keeping board members sharp and engaged – and boards resilient – will be a challenge and an opportunity for the next generation of governance leaders. How can boards boost their odds of success?

Rethink Meetings

The twentieth-century way of conducting board meetings is not up to the challenge of twenty-first-century digital transformation. Think about it: You have hundreds of pages of board documents that are often heavy on the detail and light on salient analysis. Directors find themselves flipping through digital or paper board books prepared weeks in advance—materials that instantly become obsolete should a cyber attack, regulatory change, activist investor maneuver, or some other breaking development occur after their circulation. The traditional board meeting structure – typically lengthy slide presentations with very little back and forth – can stifle open, candid, action-oriented discussion. Today's environment of rapid change, by contrast, demands distributing just the right amount of information at the right time and empowering real-time decision making.

Netflix has implemented a new way of getting more out of board meetings. A few days before a meeting, board members receive a short online memo for self-directed study that generally takes four to six hours to absorb.[10] Directors can ask questions and comment within the electronic document before and during the meeting. Executives can answer questions and amend the text as needed. Other companies have changed course similarly. According to Pamela Coles, the board and management of Rolls-Royce went through an extensive overhaul of the format, length, and focus of management's reports to the board, based on feedback on what board members want and what will save them time.

Through digital tools and procedural adjustments, boards can empower more efficient meeting preparation, discussion, and follow-up. Directors should be cautioned not to get too fixated on reducing meeting length, however. A shorter meeting isn't always a better meeting. Focus on maximizing the value of meeting time, rather than racing too quickly to the final "adjourned!"

Corporate director Margaret Whelan cited her experience on the board of a national housing company. "For two days every quarter we sit and brainstorm about business and strategy. I think that's so much more valuable [than short meetings]. There's no one who doesn't have a seat at the table, because there's so much engagement, you just can't get away with being 'checked out.'"[11]

Empower Stronger Decision Making Year-Round

The quest for more resilient board performance extends beyond the quarterly meeting. "The expectations of board directors are increasing. It almost feels as if every day you wake up you'll read about a new board member responsibility," said corporate director Nora Denzel, who serves on the boards of AMD, Ericsson, and Talend Software. "As Directors we need [to] continuously develop and improve, and technology can help us."[12]

Online tools can make information easy to find and decisions easy to track. They can also streamline scheduling, document exchange, and collaboration. (An important caveat: these tools *must* be secure.) But technology is only one piece of the board performance puzzle, Denzel cautioned.

Underlying processes need to be architected with efficiency and productivity in mind. Committees must be easy to set up, manage, and disband. Not only must the right people be in the room, they must be empowered to communicate in an environment of trust and candor. "If there is a community component, it needs to be absolutely confidential and directors can't be identified by their comments," she said.

"People, process, and technology – you need to have the three together."

Whelan cited Wells Fargo, where fake customer accounts led to $1 billion in fines, and GE, which was delisted from the Dow Jones after 110 years. "We can look at those companies and ask, 'How did it get so bad so quickly?' There were so many smart people, but there was real atrophy in the business model."[13]

A Next-Gen Take on Board Resilience[14]

Erin Lantz, Vice President and General Manager, Mortgages for Zillow Group, director on the board of directors of TrueCar, Inc., and former director on the board of directors of Washington Federal.

What steps can boards take to become more resilient?

First, be open to reevaluating your board's composition. Even though it's fairly well understood that diversity improves company outcomes, bring in real statistics so board discussions are grounded in the data. The CEO, chair, and heads of the nominating and governance committee have particularly important voices in this conversation, and can set the tone for changing processes, but it's not just their responsibility. All board members can and should contribute and champion these conversations as the board builds its pipeline and identifies diverse candidates in its network to bring into the search process.

As the board expands its candidate pipeline to include a more diverse slate of candidates, boards should also consider next-gen candidates to bring in new perspectives. Younger, tech-focused board members can bring points of view that are critical to have around the table.

What impact do you believe you've personally made as a female, next-gen director?

On both of my boards, I'm the only next-gen board member. I'd like to believe that other directors feel that I bring a useful perspective to the board – one that was previously absent. I bring my current experience as an operating executive at a high-growth tech company, a different network, and a unique lens to evaluate our growth strategy. For these reasons, I end up proposing different questions for management to consider.

At what stage should boards start thinking about diversity?

An assumption exists that diversity of thought or diversity of composition only become important at a later level of board maturity. While board size is often smaller early on, and there may be fewer opportunities to add folks with different points of view, I do think it's possible and important to make diversity a priority from the start. At a well-known online messaging company, one of the earliest hires was a female developer. This may not seem like a big deal, but this early hire created a ripple effect and attracted others. The company became known as a great place to work for diverse engineers. In my opinion, it's really a missed opportunity to wait.

Resilience through Board Composition

We've examined ways to optimize how your board works. Now let's look at *who* you choose to put on your board. This, too, is a powerful strategy for resilience.

Ideally, boards should have many voices at the table. When directors represent a diverse range of backgrounds, skillsets, and experience, organizations are more likely to spot – and call out – a potentially disastrous decision. By contrast, with a more homogenous group, such a decision stands a greater chance of being blindly accepted and rubber-stamped.

Decision-making traits across Board Behavioral Profiles have been outlined in greater detail in Chapter 7. Overall, when board members perceive themselves as strategic partners, rather than guardians of oversight or "check the box" functionaries, they structure their conversations and agendas through this lens. They proactively seek out different types of information – notably views and perspectives different than their own.

Often, in our observation, this enables boards to achieve a deeper level of understanding on how members arrived at a given decision, which is valuable if a decision leads to a beneficial result and even more valuable if it does not. Because these strategic partners have thought through an issue with this degree of comprehensiveness, they're often better able to bounce back from setbacks than other types of boards.

Greater board diversity is becoming a must rather than a "nice to have" in an era of the #MeToo movement, activist investors, and stricter diversity stances by large institutional investors.[15] In 2017, State Street Global Advisors voted against reelecting directors at about 400 companies for diversity reasons. Glass Lewis, which provides advisory services to institutional investors, announced that in 2019 it will start recommending that investors vote against the nominating committee chairs of companies with no female directors.

I was on a panel with older white men where I suggested that we should consider establishing a required minimum balance of female and male directors. One of the male panel members reacted to the idea with hostility, saying, "I would never have been on a board if that was the case." But that is what most women directors experience.[16]

– Margaret Whelan

A 2017 National Association of Corporate Directors board governance survey[17] indicates gaps between today's more homogenous status quo and the goal of more diverse boards. Despite 52 percent of directors and executives expressing a desire for more diverse candidates, 39 percent said they had difficulty finding unique skillsets and backgrounds.

Diverse perspectives make a board more relevant, resilient, and innovative. Here are some thoughts on how to foster board diversity.

Use Tools to Mind the Gaps – and Test Assumptions

Where do gaps lie in your board's current perspectives? Create a matrix to provide a full view of the board's skills and knowledge: M&A experience, views on emerging markets, knowledge of generational or demographic trends, and ability to identify and mitigate risk.

Board evaluations can help companies create a "profile" of the current board's skills and industry expertise, and identify any gaps that incoming candidates might fill. This is particularly helpful in the area of succession planning. Should a C-Suite executive or director make a sudden and unexpected departure, companies that are prepared will have a clear picture of their board's needs and will scramble less to find a replacement.

As corporate director Dr. Anastassia Lauterbach points out, "Boards need to do better jobs crafting their board profiles and understanding the areas they need to strengthen. If the board is looking for cybersecurity expertise, for example, it's important to understand the types of business questions the board wants to address and find an expert in these specific areas. Someone who understands how to protect networks might not be the right person for harnessing technological innovation for competitive advantage."[18]

Explore New Talent Sources

Don't limit the search for new directors to the board's existing networks. "Board members who rely solely on their existing network to identify new candidates may find that those networks look a lot like the board members themselves. That's why a skills matrix, formal or informal, can be a helpful tool to objectively identify the experiences and competencies desired in new board members," said Erin Lantz, Vice President and General Manager, Mortgages, for Zillow Group. "Beyond that, there's a lot that individual board members can do personally to expand their own networks and ensure the inclusion of more diverse candidates. Board members can leverage new resources like theBoardlist, ask for input from organizations like Next Gen Board Leaders, network with board members from other boards at director education conferences, and reach out to venture capitalists (VCs) who are well connected to tech operating executives and private company board members. More diverse candidates will bring along their own networks, which can also create a nice cycle of opening up board referrals."

Reconsider the criteria for new directors. Corporate director Margaret Whelan reports that in the homebuilding industry, "There are so many challenges we could never have anticipated, like the dramatic impact of the recent U.S. trade tariffs on housing affordability, the lack of availability of skilled labor. Much-needed innovation may not come from a retired CEO unless they can demonstrate they've worked in this area before."[19]

As for finding board members with the right skills and perspectives? Whelan recommends bypassing headhunters for a more personal approach. "I go to networking events to meet people and connect on a more personal level. I believe good boards are more proactive in lining up who they're going to need and that outsourcing this search to a third party is not as attractive as a board identifying a great candidate itself."[20]

Focus on Diversity's Advantages

Of course, even advanced technology, broader searches, and candidate test runs will yield limited results if a company's culture isn't supportive. Stefanie K. Johnson, associate professor of management and entrepreneurship at the University of Colorado's Leeds School of Business, researched CEO attitudes toward diversity in board recruiting.[21] CEOs who pushed for diversity focused more on the benefits diversity would bring. CEOs who did not push for board diversity were more fixated on the risks, such as a board member's being perceived as a "token" or a disrupter of group dynamics.

According to corporate director Betsy Atkins, "There isn't a single business that isn't going to be impacted by technology, and so I think that every board needs to have a core of two or three digital directors. They also need to have a global perspective, particularly if the company is multinational. Retail might be an exception – concepts like Costco, which require big SUVs and lots of storage, don't translate well from North America to Europe – but most other industries are multinational."[22]

For finding these more diverse directors, expand beyond existing networks and search firms to universities, alumni networks, finance and venture capital communities, and other companies, in and outside of your industry.

Leveraging Diverse Viewpoints to Stay Ahead of Change[23]

Betsy Atkins, CEO and founder of Baja Corporation, and director on the boards of directors of Cognizant, Wynn Resorts, SL Green Realty, Schneider Electric, and Volvo Cars.

How do you build a truly resilient board?

The way to keep a board strong and resilient is to promote board diversity. You certainly want directors with industry-specific knowledge – that's a given – along with financial experts who can chair the audit committee. But what matters most is how you keep up with the rate of change. For this, the board needs a global perspective, an international perspective, and digital savviness, plus the ability to weave together these different viewpoints.

How can companies ensure that these diverse directors get the right amount of information, at the right time?

When I chair committees, or if I'm the lead director or board chair, I invite speakers to meet with the board for working dinners. I think you build camaraderie with a deep-dive working dinner, ordering in food at the company's head-quarters where you bring in two or three speakers. Tackle a big challenging topic like digital transformation and get somebody from McKinsey or Bain or Booz Allen to come in and discuss how it applies to your company.

To me, those are the ways you get the board engaged and excited and processing as a team and understanding the external dynamics that are going to affect the business.

Start Building a Resilient Board Now

Companies can't wait until a crisis looms to start thinking about board resilience. As new business models and technologies emerge, the 10-person startup – or a well-established firm with thousands of employees – can become the next Uber or Airbnb in just a few years, if not months. The journey will be different depending on the size and newness of the firm and its Board Behavioral Profile.

"At the founding stage, the board might be very engaged – but there are few or no committees, no documentation, and no tech tools like board portals," said corporate director Laurie Yoler.[24]

A startup might have the luxury (or challenge) of building the infrastructure, tools, processes, and board diversity for resilience from scratch. Meanwhile, more established firms might have some structures in place already, but they might have to contend with change management issues as they move to a new way of operating.

Key Takeaways on Resilience

- **Put the structures and processes in place to spot risks before they become crises.** These include encouraging and accepting constructive criticism, thinking critically, fostering respectful inquiry, seeking diverse options, and remaining open to change.

- **Conduct annual anonymous evaluations, whether they're required or not.** Yes, including measuring individual director performance.

- **Always seek to self-educate and improve.** This includes being aware of the macro trends happening within and outside of your own industry.

- **Digitize your board meetings.** Electronic documents and nontraditional meeting structures can help foster candid, action-oriented discussion.

- **Bring diverse voices to the board table.** A range of backgrounds, skillsets, and expertise helps boards to identify potentially disastrous decisions. Create a skills matrix to identify what you're looking for, and network to find it yourself through universities, alumni networks, finance and venture capital communities, to name a few, outside of your industry.

Notes

1. Excerpts from telephone interview with Betsy Atkins, 21 Aug. 2018.
2. Excerpt from telephone interview with Margaret Whelan, 24 July 2018.
3. Excerpt from telephone interview with Laurie Yoler, 2 Aug. 2018.
4. Excerpts from telephone interview with Betsy Atkins, 21 Aug. 2018.
5. Excerpt from telephone interview with Laurie Yoler, 2 Aug. 2018.
6. *Global and Regional Trends in Corporate Governance for 2018*, Russell Reynolds, 2018, http://www.russellreynolds .com/en/Insights/thought-leadership/Documents /RRA%20-%20Global%20and%20Regional%20Trends%20 in%20Corporate%20Governance%20for%202018.pdf.
7. "Back to Basics: Why the Board Evaluation Is a Critical Building Block," *Boardroom Resources*, https:// boardroomresources.com/insight/board-evaluation -critical-building-block/.
8. Excerpts from telephone interview with Betsy Atkins, 21 Aug. 2018.
9. Excerpt from telephone interview with Merline Saintil, 3 Aug. 2018.
10. David F. Larcker and Brian Tayan, "How Netflix Redesigned Board Meetings," *Harvard Business Review*, 8 May 2018, https://hbr.org/2018/05/how-netflix-redesigned -board-meetings.
11. Excerpt from telephone interview with Margaret Whelan, 24 July 2018.
12. Excerpt from telephone interview with Nora Denzel, 6 Sept. 2018.
13. Excerpt from telephone interview with Margaret Whelan, 24 July 2018.
14. Excerpts from telephone interview with Erin Lantz, 9 Aug. 2018.
15. *Global and Regional Trends in Corporate Governance for 2018*, Russell Reynolds, 2018, http://www.russellreynolds .com/en/Insights/thought-leadership/Documents

/RRA%20-%20Global%20and%20Regional%20Trends%20 in%20Corporate%20Governance%20for%202018.pdf.

16. Excerpt from telephone interview with Margaret Whelan, 24 July 2018.

17. *2017–2018 NACD Public Company Governance Survey*, National Association of Corporate Directors, 2018, https:// www.nacdonline.org/files/2017%E2%80%932018%20 NACD%20Public%20Company%20Governance%20Survey %20Executive%20Summary.pdf.

18. Excerpt from telephone interview with Anastassia Lauterbach, PhD, 15 Aug. 2018.

19. Excerpt from telephone interview with Margaret Whelan, 24 July 2018.

20. Ibid.

21. Stefanie K. Johnson, "What Amazon's Board Was Getting Wrong About Diversity and Hiring," *Harvard Business Review*, 14 May 2018, https://hbr.org/2018/05/what -amazons-board-is-getting-wrong-about-diversity-and -hiring?autocomplete=true.

22. Excerpts from telephone interview with Betsy Atkins, 21 Aug. 2018.

23. Ibid.

24. Excerpt from telephone interview with Laurie Yoler, 2 Aug. 2018.

CHAPTER 3

The Board's Expanding Role in Managing Risk

B oard resilience is particularly important in today's volatile, transparent, and risk-filled business environment. What leadership doesn't know – or fails to act upon – can hurt tremendously. Take, for example, the willful violation of emission standards that resulted in more than 30 lawsuits, a 40 percent drop in stock value, and the removal of the CEO at Volkswagen. Or consider how five public pension funds have joined a lawsuit against officers and directors of Wynn Resorts Ltd.[1] The allegation: board members were aware of former CEO Steve Wynn's ongoing sexual misconduct – including harassment, abuse, and assault of employees – but failed to take action.

CEOs, chief risk officers, board members, and others are being sued, shamed, and removed from their positions for what's happened under their watch. With boards tasked to take ownership of a growing roster of risks, directors have been tasked to up their risk management skills, sooner rather than later.

Rising to the fore are cyber threats, which have exploded since 2017. Cyber attacks have grown increasingly sophisticated, as have the regulations enacted in response to these new threats. For example, the EU General Data Protection Regulations (GDPR) enacted in May 2018 to unify regulation in the EU around data privacy had significant security and compliance implications for companies around the world.[2] Violations could potentially cost a company as much as 4 percent of its annual revenue in fines.

As corporations and their boards grapple with change, the world is watching. In the security realm, Wall Street analysts can now evaluate companies' "cyber-risk ratings," which use a FICO-like score to communicate a company's vulnerability to a data breach, through tools like BitSight and Security Scorecard.

How can directors get – and stay – up to speed on changes and threats? What are the best ways to spot red flags before they become trouble? And how can boards and management best work together to take action in a timely fashion?

We suggest examining your Board Behavioral Profile, knowing and tracking the most pressing threats, and being ready for trouble before it happens.

Evaluate Your Board's Approach to Risk

Startup companies have a world of opportunity ahead of them. Governance-wise, however, they are open to a variety of vulnerabilities.

Organizations less than 10 years old are more likely to exhibit the behaviors of a Foundational Board, as we'll discuss further in Chapter 7. Directors may have limited governance experience, with minimal tools and documentation for support. Foundational Boards typically take their lead from – rather than question – management, and efficiency is typically the focus. The informal nature of proceedings and presence of few, if any, independent directors, can make consensus the norm – and stifle inquiry or dissent.

But startups don't remain startups forever, and their governance practices need to mature with their evolving risks. Take, for example, the ride-sharing phenomenon Uber, founded in 2009. In 2017, the company had 14,000 employees and more than 1 million drivers. The company also was under investigation by the U.S. Attorney General for failing to adequately investigate employee reports of sexual harassment.[3]

Co-founder Travis Kalanick stepped down from his post as Uber CEO – but was allowed to remain on the board with control over three board seats and in September 2017 appointed two new board members.[4] Furthermore, according to a complaint filed by an early Uber investor, Kalanick withheld important, relevant information about what was happening with the company before the board voted to control these seats.

A board with a strong culture of inquiry and dissent, with mutual but not blind trust, could have identified, and potentially mitigated, these issues. Furthermore, a board with more governance experience might have handled the Kalanick situation through a lens of "what could potentially go wrong?" rather than "are we checking off the right boxes?"

That said, approaching risk as merely an issue of "compliance" is insufficient. At first glance, it seems a compliance focus would be ideal for risk management, by emphasizing formalized processes, adding more independent directors, and utilizing online tools for compliance requirements such as online resolutions, voting, minutes, and board evaluations.

But even these tactics won't catch or address all risks. If directors are asking questions, but are still getting all the answers from management, they can miss important signs if management is the problem in the first place.

Directors of leading organizations take a more active role, assuming strategic partnerships or even coaching relationships with executive management. They're seeking out the big picture, with information from third-party sources. They're asking detailed questions – and challenging the answers, particularly if short-term gains come with increased risk. They're better positioned to catch and address risks in today's volatile, uncertain, complex, and evolving environment.

In the words of corporate director Margaret Whelan, "Growth should not be the [only] strategy. There's no point growing if you're not delivering an attractive return of capital and managing risk."[5]

Checklist: Tools and Tactics to Borrow and Use

Boards can bolster their risk management with proactive practices, including:

- Supplementing management reports with third-party data
- Using scorecards to evaluate compliance, risk, and board effectiveness
- Collaborating between meetings with secure online communication tools
- Educating directors on risk issues such as diversity and environmental issues (addressed later in this section)
- Networking with peers in other organizations and industries

Triage and Track Threats

You don't necessarily need to know the derivation of every phishing attack, but you need to know what phishing is.[6]

– Laurie Yoler

With risk, according to technology executive Ralph Loura, "There is often sort of a gray area. Management might say, 'Gee, it hasn't crossed this certain threshold,' so management makes a decision that they're not going to share information. And then later they're forced to share the news and then they look bad because it's been three weeks between the breach and notification."[7]

In its oversight role, a corporation's board of directors holds the power to escalate a concern to a corporate priority, call an investigation, and insist upon action. When applying this oversight to risk management, the first challenge is knowing where to look. The second is monitoring the risk landscape as thoroughly as possible without getting tangled in the weeds.

Loura recommended that the board "get involved in that conversation while it's still an abstract thought. Then you can think it through, you can provide input, and you can be more prepared rather than trying to do it in real time."[8]

Risk can take many forms: political, economic, legal, and environmental, to name a few. A rising threat area for corporations of all sizes and sectors is cyber risk – and the consequences for not effectively managing it can be catastrophic.

"We are in the midst of an accelerating and daunting pace of change, in both new cyber-related threats and new technologies that are impacting the normal course of doing business," said corporate director Merline Saintil. Guidance for boards in the evolving area of cyber risk has long been uncharted. "At least before the *NACD Cyber-Risk Oversight Handbook* came out recently, it was hard to codify best practices to follow as a board member."[9]

Technology is a double-edged sword, however. IT can also be a powerful tool for spotting and mitigating this risk – up to a certain point. Myriad software solutions, if properly managed, can help organizations collect and make sense of information. Think sensors, spreadsheets, graphs, and data analytics, plus mobile dashboards, online desktops, and interactive documents that enable real-time intelligence, as well as collaboration and notification.

Even the most advanced tools, however, might not convey important nuances or hunches derived from personal observation or past experience. Dashboards and analytics mean little without knowledge of overarching context. And many sensitive and challenging issues can't be discussed outside the boardroom or documented in writing.

As discussed elsewhere in this book in relation to value creation, strategy, and more, sometimes there's no substitute for face-to-face conversations – with management, key departments like security and R&D, investors, and others. For risk management, these interactions might be the most effective (or only) way to spot "unknown unknowns" emerging on the horizon.

When IT tools combine with interpersonal interactions, the results can be powerful. McKinsey examined tactics used in the oil and auto industries, sectors where an explosion or a product recall can have devastating consequences.[10] For one company, safety reports from field operations triggered in-depth conversations about problems and possible actions.

Nelson Chan, board chair with Adesto Technologies and board member for Deckers Outdoor Corporation, said of his experiences: "We have a review of cyber risk and tech issues at every board meeting. We're looking at a dashboard that shows incidents related to cyber-security, like phishing attempts, the success rates of those attempts, and how we're mitigating them."[11]

Loura added, "Educating the board on personal security, like the risk of using public Wi-Fi hotspots, is a good way to help them get more comfortable and extrapolate the topics to their businesses."[12]

Corporate director Merline Saintil shared the following overarching advice: "Stay humble, continue to learn, and be vigilant as risks – especially cyber risks – are dynamic and constantly changing."[13]

Boards Step Up Their Cyber Game[14]

Ralph Loura, technology advisor for REL Advisory, former chief technology officer of Rodan + Fields, and former chief information officer for Hewlett-Packard's Enterprise Group and The Clorox Company.

How do you view the board's role in overseeing cyber risk?

I think boards increasingly understand that cyber is a risk management issue that affects the whole company and requires board oversight. I don't think that was always true. Boards either had a broad appreciation of that role, or they appreciated it because they didn't want to end up on the cover of *The Wall Street Journal*. Boards have to view cybersecurity as an enterprise risk, not an IT topic, with regular briefings by management on critical

---

(continued)

updates, progress, changes, and challenges along the way. In general, boards now have a better appreciation for the space. They increasingly understand their role in oversight, requirements for budget and staffing, and the need for a regular cadence and framework with management.

Should boards bring on a cyber expert?

In general, boards should enlist an outside expert – it could be one of their existing third-party advisors or a law firm or big consulting group – to explain technology best practices and educate directors on their responsibilities and preparedness. Increasingly we see boards looking at their own makeup to ensure that they have appropriate board experience in cyber, technology, and related areas.

Adding directors with more digital experience to the board makes sense, and I'm certain a lot of boards are making that move already. But I would caution the board to be careful about how they view that person, how they recruit them, and the role they play. You don't want them to become the board equivalent of the A/V techie who's only called in for technology conversations and not listened to or engaged in a direct way in the other aspects of the company. The reality is you're recruiting a new board member who should be fully integrated into the board in a complete way, not just for digital.

Should the CIO or CISO report to the board rather than the CEO?

I don't think that makes sense. It could warp the way the strategy is pursued. The CIO in particular should report to the CEO. There is a debate on who the CISO should report to – if not the CEO, should it be the COO or CFO or someone outside of IT? The CISO should have an independent level of reporting, in the sense that their agenda or reality shouldn't be shaped by the CIO's priority or influence. On the other hand, operationally, the CISO needs to be very tightly ingrained with the CIO, and they need to be in lockstep operationally in how they deploy and manage tools and monitor and so on. Either way, there should be a level of coordination and alignment between the two and a level of independence. This can be achieved through reporting relationships or through a dotted line where the CISO also reports to the head of enterprise risk, who may be the chief legal officer or CFO.

Should Your Audit Committee Delegate Cyber Risk?

With the 2006 International Financial Reporting Standards and increased scrutiny due to the 2008–2009 financial crisis, audit committees have been shouldering risk management responsibilities beyond the financial realm – operational, technological, reputation, fraud, tax, and litigation risk, and beyond.[15]

More and more, the audit committee's responsibilities have expanded to include cybersecurity. But should they? "We just had this discussion on one of my boards," said Yoler. "Do they need a tech or cyber expert on the board? Should we create a technology committee, and does it take things off the audit committee's plate and/or the full board's plate?"[16]

Best practices around cyber risk are still evolving, but there will never be one right way to structure board oversight. Rather, today's board must make decisions about who should "own" cyber risk based on the industry in which they operate, previous cyber threat history, existing board skillsets, current committee structures, and so on. (A review of their Board Behavioral Profile, as described in Chapter 7, might be helpful as well.)

Boards can strengthen their risk management overall through:

- Regularly reviewing reports on threats, attempts, and security measures
- Allotting enough time on board meeting agendas for discussion of cyber-risk issues
- Delivering ongoing training and support around cybersecurity to help ensure directors don't become sources of risk
- Conducting annual security audits
- Developing a cyber-crisis response plan at the board level and testing it at least annually

Checklist: Collaboration with the CIO/CISO

How can board members work with the CIO/CISO to stay on top of threats and manage risks? Tips follow from Ralph Loura:[17]

- **Build a rapport with your CIO and CISO.** Encourage them to keep you apprised of developments, not just in the company but in the industry at large.
- **Ask questions.** Encourage the CIO/CISO to share insights about emerging patterns and the risk management landscape. Don't be afraid to ask questions you might think are naïve. These can produce some of the best conversations. Start with "What am I protecting? Is it reputation? Data? Your customers' personal information? Are you 'walking the talk'?" For example, if you're saying that customer information is your most valuable asset, but you're not spending much time and energy protecting customer data; you're not walking the talk. Then,

ask how the company has allocated resources to protect these strategic assets. Is there an enterprise-wide risk management framework in place with adequate staffing and budget? Ask about potential vulnerabilities and what management is doing to extend security beyond your four walls.

- **Shift your perceptions.** Boards for many decades viewed CIOs as back-office people who helped automate things or run expensive management systems. They were brought in periodically for specific topics but not really viewed as a resource for strategy. This is changing in direct correlation to the digitization of all sectors. Now the CIO is viewed as having key experience that can help in conversations around things like digital disruption for traditionally non-digital industries.

Be Ready for Anything (Because It Will Probably Happen)

When trouble hits – it could be an environmental incident, a network outage or other business disruption, executive scandal, or something new your board has not yet anticipated – customers, stakeholders, investors, and activists will expect action, led from the top.

How can you as a director or other governance professional work with management to respond accordingly? In the words of the Boy Scouts, "Be Prepared." And this preparedness starts with a plan.

Let's take ransomware as an example. These cyber attacks, in which criminals take over company networks and data and hold them "hostage" for a fee, have multiplied in damage costs 15-fold since 2015. By 2019, another business will fall victim to ransomware attack every 14 seconds, according to an October 2017 report by Cybersecurity Ventures.[18]

- How would your organization know if an attack hit?
- How would you know that your systems have been compromised?
- What would the damage be to your operations if access to your data was unavailable for a period of days or weeks?
- Who would be responsible for communicating with regulators, media, employees, customers, investors, and stakeholders?
- How would you minimize the impact on business and the bottom line (in other words, do you have a plan for business continuity/disaster recovery)?

Directors, who have fiduciary responsibility for the health of their corporations, are part of this response – they need to make sure that they can answer these questions and work with management in a timely, effective plan. (In terms of timely action, the EU Commission's GDPR and other similar regulations in the United States demand a response within 72 hours.) This plan needs to be written, and – perhaps more importantly – this plan needs to be tested to make sure it works.

One increasingly popular way of ensuring emergency preparedness involves tabletop exercises. These drills, long used in industries like oil and gas, usually involve half-day or full-day walk-throughs of various crisis scenarios[19] – but even shorter tabletop exercises can be effective. Some regulators have been encouraging them. The U.S. Treasury, for instance, has conducted cybersecurity tabletops with global financial firms, developed a robust series of exercises with other federal and state regulators, and created a tabletop exercise template for small and mid-size financial institutions.

Beyond immediate crises, governance professionals need to work with management to risk-proof the corporation as much as possible.

"One of the most important things the board should be doing is ensuring there's a response plan and that it's been tested," said technology executive Ralph Loura. "The board should review management's response plan, and you don't have to be a cybersecurity expert to understand crisis management."[20]

Finding and Cultivating the Right People

Leverage talent development and training that respond to areas of emerging risk. Think skillsets in cybersecurity, regulatory compliance, technological innovations like artificial intelligence and Internet of Things (IoT), even geopolitics. Sometimes the most valuable perspective can be from a director who's lived through a certain type of disruption, crisis, or digital transformation at another company.

Loura provided tips for those on the management side. "My advice to other CIOs or CISOs briefing their boards is to give very straightforward, frequent, regularly scheduled updates. Always speak in terms of business, risk, preparation, and so on. Stay out of the technical weeds as much as possible. Most important – and I can't stress this enough – don't try to sugarcoat or spin a situation for the board. Be fair, be candid, let them understand what you've done, where you still have risk, and why the risk still exists. Maybe it's intractable, maybe it requires more resources. Your role is to make the company better, not the board happy."[21]

Implementing the Right Processes

This may involve data management (defining how information is stored, where, how long, and who gets access) and device management (understanding how laptops, phones, and tablets are used and how they could be gateways into the corporate network). Boards need to work with management to ensure the ongoing auditing, monitoring, and updating of these processes to spot gaps and ensure effectiveness.

Corporate director Nelson Chan talked about the use of a cyber committee in this role. "The committee's role is similar to the audit committee or comp committee: They are tasked to spend 1–2 hours before every board meeting to review the details with experts, then report the summary to the board and seek decisions. They can help assess where the company is starting from and maybe coordinate a security audit and penetration testing. Then they assign a score so the board has something to review and suggest a course of action."[22]

Chan continued: "This committee can help assess the valuable assets that might be at risk, test the plan, and report back to the board. Do we have the right level of protection? Do we have a plan for response? Do we have insurance? Are we monitoring and reviewing the situation?"[23]

Loura emphasized the necessity of thorough and demanding questions. "Boards should be looking at the response plan and asking management: Under what circumstances will there be a public announcement? Do we need to send a notice to all customers? In what circumstances will we contact law enforcement? In a breach, will we bring in a third party for forensics? Have you done tabletop exercises, and have you trained for this? How comfortable are you with reacting to this?"[24]

Examine your cyber-risk insurance coverage (and your Directors & Officers coverage):

- What coverage does it provide for events like data breaches?
- Does it require a written cybersecurity policy and incident response plan? What documentation must you complete to be in compliance?
- Does the policy address your corporation's unique risk profile?
- Does the policy reflect the latest threats, regulations, and technological developments in this constantly evolving area?

Finally, after the crisis and response, conduct a postmortem: What best practices did you learn? What would you have done differently? As one example, the president and CEO of Hancock Health[25] wrote a blog post, "The Cyber Attack from the POV of the CEO," that documented an attack, response, and recovery in great detail, which both serves as an example of leadership transparency and serves as a valuable document for future reference.

Key Takeaways on Risk Management

- **Have conversations about risk management before the worst happens.** Creating a plan early on, writing it down, and testing it while there's time to think decisions through is invaluable in moments of crisis.
- **Don't be afraid to dissent.** A board that's not afraid to challenge one another and ask questions is better prepared to identify and mitigate risks.
- **Combine IT tools and interpersonal interactions.** Spotting abstract dangers on the horizon takes advantage of the innovation of sensors, spreadsheets, graphs,

data analytics, mobile dashboards, and more, in addition to conversations with management, key departments, investors, and others.

- **Add directors with more digital experience.** But treat them like complete members of the board rather than people who are only called in for technology conversations.

- **Consider a director who has already experienced a crisis.** Sometimes the most valuable perspective can be from a director who's lived through a disruption or digital transformation at another company.

The Board's Evolving Role in the Digital Age[26]

Nelson C. Chan serves as a director on the boards of directors of Adesto Technologies (where he serves as chairman); Affymetrix, Inc.; Deckers Outdoor Corporation; Outerwall Inc.; and Synaptics. Chan is also a member of the boards of directors of several privately held companies.

Tech is changing at a very rapid pace. What impact is this having on the work of directors?

Big data has become a major factor for companies. You can now easily get data on operations, customers, Common Access Card, anything you want to know. But what matters is deciding what you want to watch and measure.

Cyber risk wasn't even a concern 15 years ago, and now it's a giant issue. We have a review of cyber risk and tech issues at every board meeting. We look at a dashboard that shows incidents related to cybersecurity, like phishing attempts, the success rates of those attempts, and how we're mitigating these situations.

What can directors do to stay current?

Inside the boardroom, you need to carve out the time to ask the big questions: What is big data? What is digital marketing? How do you go to market in this digital age that's different than it was five years ago? This is as important, if not more important, than dealing with audit or compensation.

Also, when I think of the best boards of the best companies, the board is very clear. They tell the management team what data they want and the metrics they want to see on a regular basis. If the directors are driving the process, they are more active and engaged and not just passively drinking from the firehose of data.

What tools would you find helpful for preparing for board meetings and staying up to speed?

If I had one location, one source of information, that could keep me current – created for me by industry, by role, by areas of interest – it would be so helpful. Right now, there are so many places you can go, and I have to seek out the information. If someone could curate this for me and provide daily, weekly, monthly dashboards, I could stay on top of each industry and the important issues.

I also would like to see 5-10 metrics with data I can review in real time. This kind of dashboard or portal could be a vehicle for sharing information in conference calls, meetings, and collaborating overall. There's a huge opportunity for how tech can change the way boards work.

How do you see the board's role changing in terms of strategy?

I've been on boards for 15 years, and I've seen a shift to boards being viewed as a strategic asset. They want

(continued)

independence and different points of view from directors, not to beat up on management but to help shape strategy. The startups aren't as evolved in terms of committees, tools, and processes, but their objective is still innovation, growth, and how to get their companies where they want them to go.

Notes

1. "After Steve Wynn Sexual Harassment Scandal, NYC Pension Funds Join Lawsuit Against Wynn Resorts' Board of Directors," Office of the New York City Comptroller Scott M. Stringer, 26 Mar. 2018, https://comptroller.nyc.gov/newsroom/press-releases/after-steve-wynn-sexual-harassment-scandal-nyc-pension-funds-join-lawsuit-against-wynn-resorts-board-of-directors/.
2. Craig Callé, "Correcting Wall Street's Cyber Blind Spot," CFO, 25 June 2018, http://ww2.cfo.com/technology/2018/06/correcting-wall-streets-cyber-blind-spot/.
3. Laurie Segall and Jethro Mullen, "Uber CEO Travis Kalanick Resigns after Months of Crisis." CNNMoney, Cable News Network, 21 June 2017, https://money.cnn.com/2017/06/21/technology/uber-travis-kalanick-resignation/.
4. Jackie Wattles, "Ousted Uber CEO Travis Kalanick Shakes up Board of Directors," CNNMoney, Cable News Network, 30 Sept. 2017, https://money.cnn.com/2017/09/30/technology/business/uber-board-travis-kalanick/.
5. Excerpt from telephone interview with Margaret Whelan, 24 July 2018.
6. Excerpt from telephone interview with Laurie Yoler, 2 Aug. 2018.
7. Excerpt from telephone interview with Ralph Loura, 23 July 2018.

8. Ibid.
9. Excerpt from telephone interview with Merline Saintil, 3 Aug. 2018.
10. Christian Casal and Christian Caspar, "Building a Forward-Looking Board," McKinsey & Company, Feb. 2014, https://www.mckinsey.com/business-functions/strategy-and-corporate-finance/our-insights/building-a-forward-looking-board.
11. Excerpt from telephone interview with Nelson Chan, 3 Aug. 2018.
12. Excerpt from telephone interview with Ralph Loura, 23 July 2018.
13. Excerpt from telephone interview with Merline Saintil, 3 Aug. 2018.
14. Excerpts from telephone interview with Ralph Loura, 23 July 2018.
15. Hugo Nanninga, Grant Clayton, Francisco Sagredo, Diederik Amery, "Time for Audit Committees to Step Up," Executive Recruitment & Global Management Consulting, EgonZehnder, 9 July 2017, https://www.egonzehnder.com/functions/financial-officers/insights/time-for-audit-committees-to-step-up.
16. Excerpt from telephone interview with Laurie Yoler, 2 Aug. 2018.
17. Content from telephone interview with Ralph Loura, 23 July 2018.
18. Steve Morgan, ed., "2017 Cybercrime Report: Cybercrime Damages Will Cost the World $6 Trillion Annually by 2021," Cybersecurity Ventures, 2017, https://cybersecurityventures.com/2015-wp/wp-content/uploads/2017/10/2017-Cybercrime-Report.pdf.
19. Avi Gesser and Zachary B. Shapiro, "More Companies Doing 'Tabletop' Exercises to Test Crisis Management," Cyber Blog, Davis Polk, 5 June 2018, https://www.dpwcyberblog.com/2018/06/more-companies-doing-tabletop-exercises-to-test-crisis-management/.
20. Excerpt from telephone interview with Ralph Loura, 23 July 2018.
21. Ibid.

22. Excerpt from telephone interview with Nelson Chan, 3 Aug. 2018.
23. Ibid.
24. Excerpt from telephone interview with Ralph Loura, 23 July 2018.
25. Steve Long, "The Cyber Attack – From the POV of the CEO," Hancock Regional Hospital, 19 Jan. 2018, https://www.hancockregionalhospital.org/2018/01/cyber-attack-pov-ceo/.
26. Excerpts from telephone interview with Nelson Chan, 3 Aug. 2018.

CHAPTER 4

Building Insights and Just-in-Time Strategies

At Intuit, we were constantly thinking about artificial intelligence and machine learning and how to apply those technologies to finances to make smarter products and easy-to-use customer experiences. For example, we worked to free up accountants by automating tasks that were repetitive so they could find time to delight their customers.[1]

– Merline Saintil

As companies examine the aspects of digital disruption that can harm them, like cyber attacks, they're concurrently focusing on the technological innovations that can propel their businesses forward. Take blockchain,[2] for instance. Employing this new method for transactions means potentially opening up internal networks to vendors and other third parties, with a degree of risk. But the benefits blockchain could bring to settlements, payments, smart contracts, and supply chain tracking might make the risks worth it – and competitive pressures might necessitate such a move forward.

Conversations about risk have been converging with conversations about strategy, coalescing into an overall need to balance both for future growth and value.

Strategy has been defined as "a science and an art," "a careful plan or method toward a goal," and "adaptations (such as behaviors and structure) that serve an important function in achieving evolutionary success."[3]

It is a concept with roots in military operations. In today's business battlefield, strategy is often the tactical means through which corporations grow, compete, and flourish. We've discussed many approaches boards are using to create value and manage risk: leveraging online tools, enlisting more diverse perspectives, planning for crises and business continuity, collaborating in and outside of meetings in new ways. But one tactic, particularly for strategy, may supersede them all.

Asking the Right Questions at the Right Time

This tactic can often yield what we call just-in-time insight. How valuable is up-to-date intelligence in today's complicated, rapidly changing environment? In a word, *very*. Just-in-time insights can decrease the risk of "should have knowns" and help corporations catch themselves in time to shift course.

As corporate director Betsy Atkins described, the furniture company IKEA began using augmented reality and gig economy provider TaskRabbit to enhance the customer experience, allowing IKEA's bricks-and-mortar stores to continue to flourish in a time when other retailers have struggled. "That's the kind of thinking of a Futurist Board that really understands how technology is changing the business," said Atkins.[4]

Today's boards have a lot to juggle: risk management, value creation, diversity, and other oversight responsibilities, but leaving strategy behind can be devastating. Examining the 100 companies with the largest stock-price losses from 1995 through 2004, a study by BCG[5] found that for nearly two-thirds (66 percent) of these companies, losses were caused by failures in the company's operations, actions by competitors, or other lapses in strategy, rather than changes in the financial landscape.

Yet many boards only address strategic vision once a year, without sufficient debate or in-depth information, according to McKinsey.[6] The consulting firm also reported directors overall spend up to 70 percent of their time on quarterly reports, audit reviews, budgets, and compliance, rather than matters critical to the future direction and health of the business.[7]

Directors recognize this scenario needs to change. Nearly 70 percent of directors surveyed by PwC[8] said that their boards need to improve their contribution to strategy development and execution. And the 2018 annual survey by Corporate Board Member and Spencer Stuart[9] of 230 board members found they were universally concerned about their inability to stay current with the acceleration of technology innovation and disruption. In a world where customer preferences, competitive forces, and cultural values can shift both rapidly and radically, this lack of confidence is concerning.

Digital Disruption and the Twenty-First Century Director[10]

John Hinshaw is a technology executive who has served in senior positions with Hewlett-Packard, Boeing, and Verizon Wireless. He currently serves on the boards of directors of Sysco, BNY Mellon, and DocuSign.

How is digital disruption changing your company?

Every company is now a technology company – either in their products and services, or the enablement of their company, or how they work with customers, suppliers, etc. You cannot operate any company of any size without having the right technology strategy and leaders, both in terms of technology and nontech functions. On top of that, you need a technology-savvy board of directors as well to provide the right counseling, questions and thoughts on the direction of the company given the tech-driven world.

What do you think makes information technology – as an area of potential risk or reward – so different from other areas of risk and opportunity?

There are different types of directors on boards. For directors who were in active management 10–20 years ago, where technology wasn't as relevant, they have a choice – either get up to speed as much as possible or rely on other board members who might have had that relevant experience. If they choose the former, there are a lot of director education opportunities on cyber security, and other areas of technology that can help them become more tech savvy. Then there are directors who are current or recent executives who ran tech firms and gained experience in that area, and they can be tremendously helpful – whether on the risk committee, audit committee, technology committee, or in general business strategy. You do need to have a blend of directors with technology expertise as well as those who have other skills and are getting up to speed on issues like cyber risk.

Why do directors find grappling with cyber-risk issues to be so challenging?

Companies have gone through an annual review process in a lot of areas of audit and risk for years, but that hasn't started to happen until recently with cyber risk. We just did a cyber-risk audit, and as it was the first time, we had to implement a new process. Our IT infrastructures were built to "compute" and not necessarily for defense. It's also very difficult to stay current on cyber risk because the threats constantly evolve. There was just an instance where 11-year-olds were able to hack into the election system. If directors start to watch what's happening, they might be surprised to see how dramatically things change from one cycle to the next in terms of where the risks are coming from and how to address them.

Then there are questions of how to approach cyber risk – should it be something that reports to the audit committee? Directly to the CEO? These questions wouldn't be asked about other areas of risk – like finance. Then there is a set of questions about how the company is managing cybersecurity – what security framework are they using, what's the patch strategy, how do they handle dealing with outdated equipment that's no longer being supported? Having expert directors that can ask these kinds of questions is so important, but it's also important to help all directors get up to speed on the areas of concern.

(continued)

How can directors stay current and deal with IT issues in a confident (and competent) way?

You have to make sure you have the right leadership governing the processes. That means asking a variety of questions. Who is the CISO, what are that person's background and credentials? Are they the best and brightest that the company can have in that role? What expertise do they have relevant to that company's specific industry – for example, the way banks approach cyber risk might need to be different from retail, or from oil/gas companies. Does that person have the ability to communicate threats and cybersecurity approaches in clear and precise terms to the board?

Then, once you have the right leader in place, you have to determine the company's culture as it relates to cyber. Does everyone understand their own role in cyber risk, and do they understand that every time they log on to the network, they are creating a potential cyber breach? Is there a culture of cyber awareness? Are examples being provided – training, exercises and examples of hacking, tests with spoof emails sent by the company to see how many might need additional training, or ethical hacking to identify vulnerabilities? It has to be part of the fabric of the company to identify and mitigate risks. These are a couple of areas directors can press on to help create that "built to last" company – it can't just be relegated to a single committee; the entire board needs to be updated frequently on what the risks are and what the company is doing to manage the risks.

How should board members protect the information they receive as directors?

Board members are not thinking enough about their personal role in creating vulnerabilities. First, we need to remind directors of their responsibility to safeguard passwords because if someone were to gain access to their secure board software they could both potentially breach sensitive data and also possibly violate SEC rules around insider trading. This responsibility must be communicated clearly and concisely to directors – most are just handed a device and asked to use it for board meetings, but without enough training, policy, and oversight on how they use the device. Second, whoever supports the board – general counsel, corporate secretary, management – has a responsibility to supply a secure portal to the board. Some boards still email PowerPoints and send emails with confidential information – that should not exist. That change has to come from the support team; while the directors can add pressure, the support team has to do the right things. Third, there needs to be a broader corporate culture that reinforces how directors communicate – that all communication should happen through a secure board portal or other secure channel – especially when highly SEC-regulated or confidential information is being discussed. This is an area that has not had enough attention.

To ask the right questions – and get the right information – for prescient strategic decisions, here are a few things for boards to try: gain situational intelligence (know what questions to ask), get out and talk to people, and examine your Board Behavioral Profile (to be covered in Chapter 7).

Know What to Ask

A complicated business environment spurs equally complex strategic questions. What new technologies offer the most potential for future investment? What business models should be considered for future growth – or flagged as threats? How should success be measured and defined?

False optimism or a lack of knowledge can be deadly. Boards today need to challenge their strategy, and identify weaknesses, by thinking like an activist. They need to actively engage in strategic questioning in the boardroom, rather than passively listening to presentations. They also need to enlist tech-savvy directors. "Technology touches every aspect of the value chain, be it customer care, HR administration, procurement, product development, and beyond," said corporate director Dr. Anastassia Lauterbach.[11]

But identifying and recruiting such talent can take time. Educating existing board members is a tactic organizations can start putting into practice right now. This education takes two forms: knowledge of internal operations and insight into the outside business environment.

Digital Age Governance Trends and How to Navigate Them[12]

Merline Saintil is a technology executive who has worked in senior positions with Intuit, Yahoo, PayPal, Joyent, and Adobe. She currently serves on the boards of directors of Banner Corporation and Nav, Inc.

What main IT trends should board members watch in terms of risk and opportunity?

Artificial intelligence is the increased collaboration between humans and robots, drones, and other cognitive tools. It is so exciting as an alumna of Carnegie Mellon where AI was invented more than 50 years ago, to see this emerging technology go mainstream. When I was at Intuit, we were constantly thinking about AI and machine learning, and how to apply those technologies to finances to make smarter products and easy-to-use customer experiences. For example, we worked to free up accountants by automating tasks that were repetitive so they could find time to delight their customers.

Other areas are the cloud, which creates storage and computing power on demand and at unlimited scale; mobility, which gives us unlimited reach; and the Internet of Things, which connects people and devices online and offline.

How can a board member keep up?

The key is to get engaged and stay engaged. As the core responsibilities of a director evolve, you don't need to be an expert or technologist in order to be effective. The goal in an oversight role is to learn enough to ask thoughtful questions and ensure the responses you get are complete and clear.

What specific board practices have you seen change because of the rapid increases in the speed of information?

Secure messaging for board members is table stakes from a security perspective. Meanwhile, the delineation is blurring between the board's role of oversight versus taking management at face value without a third-party validation. This can be seen in the five principles for cyber security developed by NACD[13] and the Carnegie Mellon Software Engineering Institute:

1. Directors need to understand and approach cybersecurity as an enterprise-wide risk management issue, not just an IT issue.
2. Directors should understand the legal implications of cyber risk as it relates to their company.

(continued)

3. Boards should have adequate access to cybersecurity experts and expertise, and discussions about cyber-risk management should be given and sufficient time on board meeting agendas.
4. Directors should expect management to establish an enterprise-wide cyber-risk management framework with adequate staffing and budget.
5. Board management discussions about cyber risk should include identification of risks to avoid, to accept, and to mitigate or transfer through insurance, as well as specific plans associated with each approach.

What else should directors do to survive and thrive in the digital age?

My advice is to stay humble, continue to learn, and be vigilant as risks, especially cyber risks, are dynamic and constantly changing. As soon as you close one door, new ones will open, thanks to new technologies like the IoT and interconnected intelligent devices, which are rapidly proliferating and increasing enterprise-wide risk.

At Rolls-Royce, board members receive reports from management, tailored for brevity and impact. "We engaged the board and instructed them to tell us what they wanted from these papers," said Pamela Coles.[14] We recommend distributing such reports digitally, well ahead of meetings, and following up with an email reminder.

For overall landscape knowledge, many board members we spoke with curate content and engage outside experts to talk about timely topics, such as AI, robotics, and other technological disruptions. Some companies connect directors to courses (online or in person) on pertinent topics, such as cybersecurity, and regularly get directors out of the boardroom to visit key facilities, like R&D, and other companies and industries.

For intelligent questions and meaningful discussions, boards must "train directors to look for market dynamics," said corporate director Betsy Atkins – and much of this learning will be self-guided as well as board-led. "Listen to earnings calls from competitors, read industry reports and information from futurists. Directors need to keep an eye on macro trends in and outside of their industries, because they're going to affect your business."[15]

Gathering information and shoring up knowledge is only the first step, however. Directors need to be able to grasp important connections: between outside forces and internal operations, corporate performance and marketplace benchmarks, status quo and future scenarios, and more.

Several dashboard tools are available in the marketplace. We've seen comparison tools[16] used by asset managers to oversee fund investments and revenue forecasters from the world of technology sales.[17] Some governance professionals suggest preset benchmarks that show progress on plans and budgets.[18] This can help board members see how management is performing against objectives and if it's time for a change in strategy or other adjustment.

Options abound. As you select what's best for your board, we have one overarching recommendation: Devote as much attention and focus to analyzing the data as you do to gathering it. Data collected just to be set aside, devoid of greater insight and business intelligence, is as useless as no data at all.

"Dashboards are extremely helpful for boards to keep an eye on performance," said Nelson Chan, board chair with Adesto Technologies and board member for Deckers Outdoor Corp. "You can now easily get data on operations, customers – anything you want to know. What matters is deciding what you want to measure and watch and getting that data in a format that is meaningful and useful for the board's role. Right now, we go into a portal and look at board material, but we could do much more. We could review dashboards and see information that's pertinent to the health of the business. There are 5–10 metrics I want to measure and see that data in real time. It becomes an important source of education."[19]

"In 15 to 20 years, boards will have access to real-time data and know how to read and interpret it," said Dr. Anastassia Lauterbach, author of a new book on business applications for artificial intelligence. "This will require a robust cloud strategy, IT architecture that maps to business demands, and the right talent, both employees and freelancers."[20]

Get Out and Talk to People

Despite a promising premise – a subscription-based movie ticket service – startup MoviePass[21] experienced challenges in execution from day one: ongoing tension with partner theaters, a competing strategic direction (collecting and selling data) from a controlling stake investor, unhappy customers, and woeful underperformance by its film financing division. (The movie *Gotti* received the first-ever 0 percent rating on the fan site Rotten Tomatoes.)[22] By July 2018, after cutting its subscription price by more than half, the company was borrowing $5 billion to pay its bills.

Just-in-time strategic insights could have helped MoviePass spot issues that were later noted retrospectively, such as lower incentives for certain viewers (people with children or in lower-cost markets), significant weaknesses in its negotiating position with theaters, and optimism about its ability to attract new funding.

Given the pace of change, we suspect that not all companies in similar situations will be able to pick up all relevant red flags with online intelligence and dashboards. There's real value to touring facilities and talking to management, getting out in the field to see customer behavior and the competitive marketplace firsthand, and meeting face-to-face with key investors, partners, and other stakeholders. And because such communication goes both ways, directors also need to move beyond annual meetings and investor relations reports for communicating current performance and future direction.

No less than the chair of the Securities and Exchange Commission has noted the importance of corporate boards as central players in shareholder engagement.[23] This amped-up outreach goes beyond the elaborate gatherings, à la Disney and Berkshire Hathaway that have become the stuff of annual meeting legend. Think of shareholder engagement in terms of frequency as well as flash. Schedule off-cycle shareholder meetings by phone or in person to discuss timely strategic opportunities and concerns.[24] Find opportunities for directors to sit in on key management and business meetings, with explicit instructions to listen and learn rather than overreach and interfere.[25] Hold board meetings in corporate locations[26] that are conducting innovative research or piloting new products or business models – and make sure to expose directors to these advancements through activities like R&D facility tours. And invite board members to travel with salespeople meeting with key accounts.

For technology executive Ralph Loura, one important perspective is internal, specifically the company's top technology executives.

"CIOs for many decades were viewed as the back-office guys who helped automate things or run expense-management systems," he said. "They were brought in periodically for occasional conversations on specific topics at board meetings, but they haven't really been viewed as strategic from a board perspective. That is changing in direct correlation to the digitization of all sectors. Now they're viewed as having a key experience set that can help in conversations around things like digital disruption for traditionally nondigital industries."[27]

Whether connecting with internal or external audiences, it's all about a commitment to lifelong learning, according to corporate director Jan Babiak. "When something new comes along, directors should invest time in it. Every board member, not just a motivated one or two, should be attending updates by organizations like NACD or a law firm or a Big Four firm. We're all learning and sharing."[28]

Technology, Strategy, and Today's Governance Professional[29]

Laurie Yoler is a strategic advisor to companies on disruptive technologies, and is a director on the boards of directors of Church & Dwight, Zoox, Bose Corporation, and Noon Home; she was a founding director on the board of directors of Tesla.

How has your board role been impacted by IT and technology?

Early on in my career at Accenture (this was back in the 1980s), I spent time working with boards in every major industry trying to explain why they should care about tech. They would find consultants to bring in expertise, but it was considered a "once in a while, nice to have thing." Today, tech firms can focus on strategy since tech is the business of the company, but nontech firms are still grappling with how often to discuss tech and whether or not to have a tech committee like a comp or audit committee. In the last year it's become more the norm to discuss these issues because tech has permeated so many industries that didn't previously need it to be successful.

Why do many directors find IT issues so challenging?

I sit on a compensation committee, and when we have a meeting, the HR exec and outside consultants bring in a ton of data on executive compensation for us for making our decisions. But in tech, the depth and breadth of the issues are so much broader, and the rapid pace of change makes it a particularly challenging area for board members to stay up to speed. For example, a manufacturing firm might focus on specific robotic systems as the most important thing, but this might change in six months.

So the tech consultants that come into the boardroom tend to be one-off speakers without the same level of engagement and longevity that you have with auditors, outside counsel, compensation consultants, and so on. These consultants don't get to know the company over time and build the trust needed to suggest strategies.

(continued)

Some consultants help companies see what new technologies might impact their industry in coming years, but it's still very broad.

Across such a broad landscape, what can directors do to stay up to speed?

The type of tech you need to know is going to differ somewhat by sector, but innovations like 3-D printing could have applications in every industry, so it's a bit of a risk to think some technology doesn't apply to you. If I'm not in the financial services industry, do I need to understand cryptocurrency? Maybe not in detail, but I'd better understand that it's important and having a giant impact. It's crucial that directors spend time becoming aware of these broad areas. *The Wall Street Journal* has a weekly update on the tech areas that directors should pay attention to, as does the National Association of Corporate Directors.

What technologies do you see altering board work?

The [board] portals are already tremendous, but so much more can be done with a portal beyond just quarterly reports – videos, educational content, videoconferencing of town hall meetings, and the more creative sharing of information between board members. And as we're seeing more tools for employee-performance management, maybe the same concept could be applied to evaluating board performance. I just saw a new tool that allowed us to see what everyone thought of each part of the presentation and gave us an entirely new insight into the meeting.

How do you see boards differing at startups versus more established companies?

On a startup board I'm on, they use the board like an extension of the executive team. They try to engage the board in every strategic conversation. At the founding stage, the board might be very engaged – but there are few or no committees, no documentation, no tech tools. In a public company, by contrast, it might be an incredibly effective board that's been together for a long time with extraordinary executives who try to benchmark themselves in every way. It's considered a well-oiled machine, but it might not be a "strategic asset" board because they don't meet that often. But the "mind-set" – the primary reason for the board to be in existence and what they see as their primary function – can change each quarter with changes in the landscape, industry, regulations, and aspirations. I've been interviewing for a number of boards. Some will tell me that they're mostly a compliance board but they're trying to focus more on growth and they need more independence and diversity. Others are Innovation Boards. They're pushing boundaries, but they need to buckle up and focus on how they're going to be more efficient.

Examine Your Board's Profile

Boards seeking to grow in their strategic role may also benefit from taking a look at the Board Behavioral Profiles highlighted in Chapter 7. By knowing the profile types that best fit your board at a given time and the dynamics associated with these profiles, you can better understand your board's strengths and weaknesses for serving in a strategy-shaping role.

Foundational Boards, particularly at very young companies, may be looking to management for strategic direction, rather than recognizing their potentially powerful role in this area. They are typically more oriented toward rubber-stamping existing strategy rather than actively asking questions about the "why?"

behind it. As directors gain knowledge, experience, and confidence, they should evolve in their strategic role. Education and guidance by more seasoned governance professionals may help.

Structural Boards will be more accustomed to asking questions. But they still tend to look predominantly to management for answers, rather than confirming or challenging findings with outside research. And their questions are typically more oriented toward the watchdog variety: What do we need to do for compliance? How can we avoid risk? Because the focus isn't on new business models, emerging technologies, and evolving customer demands, such boards may be more limited in their ability to deliver strategic guidance about creating value.

Catalyst Boards, by contrast, recognize their role in company growth. They actively seek data, analysis, and insights for asking better questions and starting to use online tools for collaboration and education. To get answers to these questions, they foster partnerships with management and stakeholders. Many network with their peers on other boards for additional wisdom and context.

Futuristic Boards consider themselves coaches as well as advisors. Here strategic discussions predominate in meetings, with directors driving the agenda, and board members regularly interacting with investors, customers, executives, and peers. Innovation and sustainability are the focus, supported by even more advanced tools such as online scorecards for board effectiveness and personalized content delivery for education. These directors recognize the evolving nature of strategic leadership and know when it's time to hand the reins to fresh leadership, in strategy and other matters.

Key Takeaways for Board Strategy

- **Be flexible in your thinking.** Risk, especially cyber risk, is constantly changing.

- **Ask questions.** That's an essential step to getting the right information at the right time for smart, timely decisions.

- **Make connections.** Use dashboard tools to read content and help grasp important connections, including between outside forces and internal operations, corporate performance and marketplace benchmarks, and status quo and future scenarios. And don't just gather the data – analyze it and use it.

- **Leverage your CIOs.** They possess valuable knowledge on risks and opportunities related to digital transformation.

- **But supplement this with your own learning.** Proactively seek out articles, courses, events, and networking opportunities to stay current on digital and business trends.

Notes

1. Excerpt from telephone interview with Merline Saintil, 3 Aug. 2018.
2. "What Corporate Boards Should Know About Blockchain," *Boardroom Resources: Inside America's Boardrooms,* 2017, https://boardroomresources.com/episode/what-corporate-boards-should-know-about-blockchain.
3. "Strategy," *Merriam-Webster,* https://www.merriam-webster.com/dictionary/strategy.
4. Excerpts from telephone interview with Betsy Atkins, 21 Aug. 2018.
5. Ulrich Pidun, Marc Rodt, Alexander Roos, Sebastian Stange, and James Tucker, "The Art of Risk Management:

CFO Excellence Series," *CFO Excellence Series*, BCG, 30 Apr. 2017, https://www.bcg.com/publications/2017/finance-function-excellence-corporate-development-art-risk-management.aspx.

6. Christian Casal and Christian Caspar, "Building a Forward-Looking Board," McKinsey & Company, Feb. 2014, https://www.mckinsey.com/business-functions/strategy-and-corporate-finance/our-insights/building-a-forward-looking-board.

7. Ibid.

8. "Directors From Time Warner, Johnson & Johnson, Wendy's to Headline 2018 Boardroom Summit in New York," Chief Executive, 14 Feb. 2018, https://chiefexecutive.net/directors-time-warner-johnson-johnson-wendys-headline-2018-boardroom-summit-new-york/.

9. "What Directors Think 2018," Spencer Stuart & Corporate Board Member, Apr. 2018, https://www.spencerstuart.com/research-and-insight/what-directors-think-2018.

10. Excerpts from telephone interview with John Hinshaw, 13 Aug. 2018.

11. Excerpt from telephone interview with Anastassia Lauterbach, PhD, 15 Aug. 2018.

12. Excerpts from telephone interview with Merline Saintil, 3 Aug. 2018.

13. Larry Clinton, "Cyber-Risk Oversight: Director's Handbook Series," National Association of Corporate Directors, and Internet Security Alliance, 2014, https://nacdonline.org/files/NACD%20Cyber-Risk%20Oversight%20Executive%20Summary.pdf.

14. Excerpt from telephone interview with Pamela Coles, 7 Aug. 2018.

15. Excerpts from telephone interview with Betsy Atkins, 21 Aug. 2018.

16. "New Morningstar Competitive Intelligence Tool—Investor Pulse—Allows Asset Managers to Better Assess the Flows Landscape," Cision PR Newswire, 22 May 2018, https://www.prnewswire.com/news-releases/new-morningstar-competitive-intelligence-toolinvestor-pulseallows-asset-managers-to-better-assess-the-flows-landscape-300652221.html.

17. Bruce Harpham, "9 Ways to Get More Value from Business Intelligence in 2018," *CIO*, 25 June 2018, https://www.cio.com/article/3254646/business-intelligence/9-ways-to-get-more-value-from-business-intelligence.html.
18. Holly J. Gregory, "Governing Through Disruption: A Boardroom Guide for 2018," Practical Law, Thomson Reuters, 2017, https://www.sidley.com/-/media/publications/novdec17_govcounselor.pdf.
19. Excerpts from telephone interview with Nelson Chan, 3 Aug. 2018.
20. Excerpt from telephone interview with Anastassia Lauterbach, PhD, 15 Aug. 2018.
21. Andrew R. Chow, "Tracking MoviePass's Bumpy History as Turmoil Continues," *New York Times*, 31 July 2018, https://www.nytimes.com/2018/07/31/movies/moviepass-timeline.html.
22. Ibid.
23. David R. Beatty, "How Activist Investors Are Transforming the Role of Public-Company Boards," McKinsey & Company, Jan. 2017, https://www.mckinsey.com/business-functions/strategy-and-corporate-finance/our-insights/how-activist-investors-are-transforming-the-role-of-public-company-boards.
24. Ethan A. Klingsberg and Elizabeth K. Bieber, "How to Avoid Bungling Off-Cycle Engagements With Stockholders," Cleary M&A and Corporate Governance Watch, Cleary Gottlieb, 17 May 2018, https://www.clearymawatch.com/2018/05/avoid-bungling-off-cycle-engagements-stockholders/.
25. David Larcker and Brian Tayan, "How Netflix Redesigned Board Meetings," *Harvard Business Review*, 8 May 2018, https://hbr.org/2018/05/how-netflix-redesigned-board-meetings.
26. Casal and Caspar, "Building a Forward-Looking Board."
27. Excerpts from telephone interview with Ralph Loura, 23 July 2018.
28. Excerpt from telephone interview with Jan Babiak, 16 Aug. 2018.
29. Excerpts from telephone interview with Laurie Yoler, 2 Aug. 2018.

CHAPTER 5

From Corporate Citizenship to ESG

Shareholders use many acronyms to gauge a corporation's value: earnings per share (EPS), return on equity (ROE), and LTV/CAC (lifetime value/customer acquisition cost), to name a few. A new one is rising in priority: ESG (environment, sustainability, and governance). And the days of ESG as "nice to have" activities to generate goodwill and feel-good PR are moving behind us. Given its power to minimize risk and maximize shareholder value, attention to ESG has become a business imperative.

"It's in the storming, forming, and norming stage right now," according to corporate director Nora Denzel. "Boards are sitting down and creating sets of criteria around diversity, carbon footprints, worker safety, and so on. Which aspects of the environment, sustainability, and governance are most relevant to their business?"[1]

Often, this relevance, and the ascendance of ESG priorities, is due to outside forces: When Arjuna Capital and As You Sow filed a resolution asking Exxon Mobil to report on how the company plans to reduce dependence on fossil fuels, they highlighted climate change as a business risk that demanded corporate attention and more transparency between the board and shareholders.[2] In March 2018, institutional investors representing $100 million of Rio Tinto's shares filed a motion to the mining giant's Australian arm to review its association memberships.[3] The charge: These groups' lobbying activities were hindering sensible climate change and energy policy and therefore jeopardizing Rio Tinto's financial position.

"Activism and active shareholders have spurred these changes in governance," said Denzel. "With external guidance from investors, boards had to retool."[4]

In addition, many organizations have seen substantial gains by integrating ESG analysis as a central part of their investment strategies. One case in point: The assets under management of the signatories on the UN Principles for Responsible Investment have grown from $6 trillion to almost $60 trillion in 10 years.[5] In another example, a group at Harvard Business School found that securities scoring higher in terms of exposure to companies with ostensibly good ESG ratings tended to post higher annualized returns.[6]

In this environment, boards are focusing on developing the processes, structures, and tools to mobilize and coordinate efforts. Where can boards start to get ahead of change – and shareholder expectations? Try focusing on the following three areas: tracking data, communicating transparently and responsively, and empowering board members as ESG ambassadors.

Tracking Data

To mitigate ill effects and guide future growth, corporations need to understand the impact of their business practices on the environment and on our society.

Increasingly, it's not just the bottom line demanding such data, it's institutional investors as well, who are factoring ESG data into corporate valuations and investment strategies.

BlackRock is particularly active, joining with J.P. Morgan to launch a new suite of ESG indices,[7] developing ESG funds for retirement savings plans,[8] and drafting an open letter to the CEOs of all publicly traded companies emphasizing the importance of leadership in ESG issues.[9] Meanwhile, Vanguard announced plans to launch two ESG-focused index ETFs.[10]

If the world's biggest investors are tracking how corporations are doing in terms of ESG, these corporations need to be tracking ESG metrics as well – and ideally getting ahead of the game in terms of depth and speed of information.

"We used to be marathon runners, and now we have to be sprinters and well-rounded athletes," said Denzel. "We've had to change from processes that carry over multiple quarters to an adaptive style of governance that can better identify atypical, disruptive risks and work faster to react and respond. Sometimes board processes need to work on the basis of minutes and hours."[11]

Tools are emerging to ease this shift. State Street clients can use the company's ESGX[SM] tool[12] to assess a company's carbon footprint, board diversity, and labor across the supply chain. The Task Force on Climate-related Financial Disclosures (TCFD) has created an online Knowledge Hub[13] featuring 300 governance, strategy, risk management, and metrics users can search by topic and resource type, which include regulatory, guidance, research, frameworks, and webinars.

Yet, thus far, no clear standard metrics or terminologies exist for evaluating initiatives and effectiveness across all areas of ESG. And comprehensive evaluation of ESG effectiveness requires both qualitative assessment on how the company can "think bigger than itself" and quantitative data to gauge the impact on the bottom line.[14]

As this area evolves and is codified, governance professionals can look to what corporate entities around the world are doing for guidance. "What Netflix does is innovative," said Denzel. "Rather than providing directors with a single batch of board materials before the meeting, the board equips directors with a shared online document they can annotate and make comments on leading up to the meeting. Management can then go back and jot notes and questions for the board. It's a living document, rather than a single download of material that has to be digested all at once."[15]

Spotlight on ESG in the UK[16]

Pamela Coles is company secretary of Rolls-Royce plc. She has held a variety of company secretary roles, including serving as head of secretariat for Centrica plc, group company secretary and executive committee member for The Rank Group plc, and company secretary and head of legal at RAC plc. Ms. Coles is a non-executive director of E-ACT, a large Multi-Academy Trust, and a fellow of the UK-based ICSA: The Governance Institute.

What is the Rolls-Royce board doing in terms of ESG?

We have just enhanced our environment committee to create an executive-level environment and sustainability committee, which is led by our head of technology and which both the chairman and I have recently joined, to ensure a strong connection to the board. We are inviting shareholders to come and engage with that committee so we can listen to them and encourage a two-way dialogue. We also publish an ESG newsletter and hold governance days where we invite investors and stakeholders.

We've been doing a lot with employees. One of our non-executive directors is our employee champion, and we have a stakeholder committee to support her. She travels across the Group and meets with many different groups of our people in order to get a broad range of views and to take every opportunity to listen to employees and their concerns and to pick up on the culture. These have included European Works Council meetings, diversity and inclusion events, meetings with our graduates and apprentices and online interactive sessions. She takes their feedback directly back to the board. This isn't a substitute for employees going through management or whistle-blowing, but it is a different way of the board listening to employees. There are a few things we're doing quite differently. We also run "Meet the Board" events where anyone can ask a question in a completely open Q&A and a "Board Apprentice" program.

Is a commitment to ESG structural or cultural?

The structure is important, but the culture is even more so. For example, the UK government came out with a number of initiatives saying we have to connect with our employees, but that's not why we did it. We did it because we needed to. You have to apply corporate governance in a way that is going to bring you benefit, rather than take a tick-the-box approach. If you do something because the regulator tells you to do it, that's not necessarily adding value at all.

(continued)

> **As the board's composition becomes more diverse, how do you get new directors up to speed and delivering value?**
>
> We look at their backgrounds and what they already know, and then we help them fill in the gaps. On our board, we have a Singaporean who is really well connected in China and U.S. directors who may not be so well briefed on UK Corporate Governance – we will shape their inductions to help fill the gaps and use others' specialist knowledge to help brief the rest of the board.

Communicating Transparently and Responsively

Once a corporation has collected this data, the next step is to share it.

Today's institutional investors and shareholders are holding boards to an unprecedented standard of transparency. Withhold information, especially about sensitive ESG issues, and you risk a proxy battle, resistance to director appointments, and other issues, particularly in today's era of the activist investor.

In March 2018, Trillium Asset Management made sure Starbucks' shareholders got the memo. Arguing that Starbucks' insufficient diversity disclosures were impacting business outcomes and company culture, the firm led a shareholder request for an annual report of diversity figures and policies.[17] Meanwhile, when Walmart changed rules for voting on wage transparency and other issues for the first time in the history of its shareholder meetings: an activist website[18] posed the question, "What is Walmart hiding?"

Disclosure, particularly about ESG issues, is a fine balance.[19] Law – and, increasingly, shareholder and public demand – require a certain degree of openness. And a court ruling of withheld or misstated information can hold significant legal and financial consequences. However, companies that reveal too much risk compromising competitive or operational advantages.

How can governance professionals determine what to share (and what to keep private) to get ahead of such requests? How can they make sure this information is communicated in a responsive, transparent fashion?

Deciding what to share is a complicated, constantly evolving issue, and every board will differ in its processes. Informed directors are the first step to success. Governance professionals should strive to make reports easy to understand for those who need to know, and to train directors on how to analyze and communicate their findings in their role as ambassadors to investors, shareholders, internal audiences, customers, and the public.

A stakeholder advisory committee, such as those used by French insurance company AXA[20] and Canadian utility IESO,[21] can help governance professionals stay in touch with current and emerging issues, particularly those related to underserved communities, diversity and social inclusion, and environmental sustainability. Look to nonprofits, NGOs, community groups, and others to enlist a wide range of perspectives. Proactively engage them during and between meetings. And genuinely listen to and respond to their concerns.

Technology solutions can support responsive, transparent communications on many levels: for information sharing, for collaboration, and for decision making through automatic voting and real-time resolutions. This "electronic paper trail" can be vital in helping a board prove its decision-making processes should an action ever be called into question.

As an overarching guideline, we encourage following the best practices of the United Nations: Communicate internally and externally to ensure that everyone understands the importance of ESG issues and what is being done to address them to lead a more transparent, ethical business practice.[22] And once you've established standards for reporting, emphasize that you're serious with disclosure practices that reflect these standards.

Empowering Board Members as ESG Ambassadors

Ideally, time spent in the boardroom should represent just a fraction of a board member's role. Directors should serve as their company's greatest evangelists outside of it as well. Unfortunately, this can be a mission easier said than done. When taking a stand on hot-button topics like climate change, immigration, LGBTQ rights, or racial or gender equality, a positive reception isn't always guaranteed. Shareholders represent the full spectrum of political opinion, after all. The repercussions for speaking out can include public backlash, boycotts, or even a disapproving tweet from the highest levels of government.

But what does such a statement do to the bottom line? *Harvard Business Review* examined daily stock prices before and after CEO statements for more than a dozen companies that took a stand on ESG issues.[23] The findings: Most companies did not see a sustained rise or fall after such statements, and those that did generally saw prices return to their usual levels after around two months.

Aron Cramer, a sustainability expert who serves on many boards, stressed in a January 2018 *Forbes* magazine interview[24] the importance of business leaders stating what they stand for – *especially* in an environment of political, economic, and technological disruption. He specifically cited the need to invest in new technologies for clean energy and to collaborate on solutions to global challenges. We fully believe that shareholders expect such statements. If your business involves natural resources, a global workforce, or serving diverse markets of customers, then silence on climate change, immigration, or discrimination can speak volumes – and not in a good way.

Technology can't lessen the stress of speaking out and potentially exposing oneself to backlash from colleagues, media, or the public after doing so. Software and apps can't develop the perfectly nuanced ESG messaging that represents both your corporate values and the current zeitgeist. This task is up to the talented minds on your board.

But online tools can make the process of speaking out easier. They can also create a more intimate connection between corporate leaders, investors, shareholders, and customers – provided the messengers are well-versed in the appropriate messages to deliver and are able to be responsive to questions in real time.

Through offering a centralized, convenient place to find the latest information (such as messaging and materials), these tools can help directors stay on top of the issues – like breaking policy and regulatory developments – and corporate messaging and materials relevant to these developments. Secure apps and online portals can facilitate conversations and information sharing for internal collaboration. Furthermore, by tracking outside conversations – such as reactions and discussions on social media – technology can help governance professionals make sure their messages are on target and not out of touch.

At Rolls-Royce, the board and management have been working in concert to refine their board papers. "People think the board wants 40 to 50 pages of deep details, but directors don't need to read the equivalent of [the novel] *War and Peace* over the weekend," said Company Secretary Pamela Coles. "We used an external company to help us write a good template and develop a good training program. We had to engage the executive team, telling them they have to own these papers. And we had to ask the board what they wanted from these papers."

"So we've done a lot of education, templates, even videos of directors saying 'this is what I want to see,'" Coles said. "Authors are not allowed to do more than half a page of executive summary, and they have to have a conclusion. We've structured board papers around the questions the board wants answered. It's a hard way to write a board paper, but it really makes people think."[25]

Checklist: Supporting Board Ambassadors

How can boards empower directors to be effective ESG ambassadors? These recommendations are from the 2016 United Nations Global Compact:[26]

- Keep a finger on the pulse of ESG issues – especially those that pertain most to your given industry.
- Communicate these issues with everyone: directors, chairpersons, CEOs, and committees. And amend your communications as issues progress or change.
- Provide sufficient time and information for the discussion of agenda items in meetings.
- Make sure all board members understand what ESG issues are and how they affect business.

Key Takeaways on ESG

- **Collect data from employees.** Actively listen to their concerns before they go to management. Holding Q&As with board members is one unique way directors can gain feedback from employees.

- **Keep directors informed.** Reports should be easy to understand, and directors should be trained on how to analyze and communicate their findings to investors, shareholders, internal audiences, customers, and the public.

- **Look outside your company.** There are plenty of corporate entities placing importance on ESG issues that can serve as models.

- **Speak out about what you stand for.** In this environment of political, economic, and technical disruption, it's crucial to let shareholders know directors' stances on the issues of the day.

- **Let tech support you.** Information sharing, collaboration, and decision making are all means of communication that can be made more transparent by technology. What's more, having a centralized place to find the latest information helps directors stay on top of the issues and the relevant corporate messaging.

Views on ESG and More from Singapore[27]

Colin Low is a global/local executive and an international board director based in Singapore who serves as chairman of the board of directors of Intraco Limited (Mainboard Singapore Exchange Listed) and Singapore Investment Development Corporation. He is

(continued)

the U.S. National Board Director for the Cancer Treatment Centers of America with regional hospitals across the United States. He also served as president of GE International's South East Asia region from 2005 to 2010 and as GE's Investment Board director for Asia Pacific operations.

What do you believe to be the primary role and value of a sustainability report?

A sustainability report is now a requirement for any company listed on the Singapore Stock Exchange, but it should be modus operandi for any company. Intrinsically, organizations should operate on a philosophy of being efficient in their use of resources like water and electricity, in their industrial processes and in daily operations. Every resource should be used at an optimum level, say generating fewer greenhouse gases or using less water, and every organization should fundamentally think this through. The company should be making a positive impact in the community it serves, creating goodwill, creating benefits, and so on.

How do you manage ESG and related initiatives throughout the year?

Coming from a GE background, I'm interested in deep process, and you have to have a clear process at the board level. For example, on the board I serve on, we start the year setting the KPIs, key measurements, and priorities for the organization, and we discuss what we're going to accomplish and our strategy for getting there.

In April, we focus on compensation and executive leadership. We review talent and their achievements in the last fiscal year, identify the emergent leaders who can come up through their divisions and even to the C-Suite level, and conduct a company-wide assessment to benchmark where talent can grow into their next position.

Mid-year, we think about how we're going to perform, not only for the second half of the year but for the next two to three years. Right now, we have two companies in the plastics industry, which is operating widely across Southeast Asia and China. The changes in oil prices and the ongoing U.S.–China trade war are having a lot of impact on the business in 2018 and beyond. In our assessment, I believe the impact will be positive and opportunistic.

In October, we reflect on compliance, sustainability, the gap of where the organization is in compliance in the regulatory environment. Singapore has new regulations around ESG, so this is the time of the year when we review how we're meeting these requirements.

Then, in December, we end the year by reviewing the gaps and actions we took throughout the year to mitigate volatility, and we approve the final budget for the next fiscal year.

Talk about what's expected in terms of personal accountability on your board.

We have very high expectations of all board members, whether they are executives or independent or representing specific shareholder groups. Our leaders expect board members to represent the full range of stakeholders, because if you have different groups pulling the board in different directions, it freezes the company, and the company cannot change or grow. In these times, boards have to be very responsive. They can't just stay still. You've got to really look at the contribution of your directors and ask if they're out for the interests of the organization. For big

(continued)

public companies, this can be very challenging because there is a lot of pressure from shareholders individually. Board directors must focus on the overall growth of the company, and the long-term well-being of the company as a whole should be at the core of each director's thinking and interests.

Notes

1. Excerpts from telephone interview with Nora Denzel, 6 Sept. 2018.
2. "Arjuna Capital & As You Sow Statement on ExxonMobil Silencing of Shareholder Resolution on Carbon Asset Transition," Arjuna Capital, 2 Apr. 2018, http://arjuna-capital.com/news/arjuna-capital-as-you-sow-statement-on-exxonmobil-silencing-of-shareholder-resolution-on-carbon-asset-transition/.
3. Michael Slezak, "Rio Tinto Won't Allow UK Investors to Vote on Mineral Council Issue." *The Guardian*, 9 Mar. 2018, https://www.theguardian.com/business/2018/mar/09/rio-tinto-wont-allow-uk-investors-to-vote-on-mineral-council-issue.
4. Excerpt from telephone interview with Nora Denzel, 6 Sept. 2018.
5. Matt Orsagh, "ESG: The Risks and Opportunities," *Ethical Boardroom*, 12 Feb. 2017, https://ethicalboardroom.com/esg-the-risks-and-opportunities/.
6. Thomas Franck, "Social and Sustainable Investing Gets a Boost from an Unlikely Source: Wall Street Activists," CNBC, 27 Apr. 2018, https://www.cnbc.com/2018/04/27/social-investing-gets-a-boost-from-an-unlikely-source-activists.html.
7. "J.P. Morgan Collaborates with BlackRock to Launch New ESG Suite of Indices: The J.P. Morgan ESG Index (JESG)," J.P. Morgan, 18 Apr. 2018, https://www.jpmorgan.com/country/GB/en/detail/1320566638713.

8. Melissa Karsh and Emily Chasan, "BlackRock, Wells Fargo Are Said to Push ESG Funds in 401(k)s," Law.com, *Daily Business Review*, 13 June 2018, https://www.law.com/dailybusinessreview/2018/06/13/blackrock-wells-fargo-are-said-to-push-esg-funds-i/?slreturn=20180528121355.

9. Larry Fink, "Larry Fink's Annual Letter to CEOs: A Sense of Purpose," BlackRock, Jan. 2018, https://www.blackrock.com/corporate/investor-relations/larry-fink-ceo-letter.

10. "ESG Investing and How Vanguard's 2 New ETFs Can Help," Fund News, Vanguard, 27 June 2018, https://investornews.vanguard/esg-investing-and-how-vanguards-2-new-etfs-can-help/.

11. Excerpts from telephone interview with Nora Denzel, 6 Sept. 2018.

12. "State Street Enhances ESG Products with New Data and Analytics Offerings," Newsroom, State Street Global Advisors, 15 Nov. 2017, http://newsroom.statestreet.com/press-release/corporate/state-street-enhances-esg-products-new-data-and-analytics-offerings.

13. Randi Morrison, "Online Resource Platform on Climate Disclosure Framework Launched," Society for Corporate Governance, 3 May 2018, https://connect.societycorpgov.org/blogs/randi-morrison/2018/05/03/online-resource-platform-on-climate-disclosure-fra.

14. "Three Ways to Improve Your Board's ESG Reporting," Boardroom Resources, 2018, https://boardroomresources.com/insight/three-ways-improve-boards-esg-reporting/.

15. Excerpts from telephone interview with Nora Denzel, 6 Sept. 2018.

16. Excerpts from telephone interview with Pamela Coles, 7 Aug. 2018.

17. "Letter to Starbucks Shareholders," Trillium Asset Management, 5 Mar. 2018, http://www.iccr.org/sites/default/files/page_attachments/2018_starbucks_memo_-_proposal_7.pdf.

18. "2018 Walmart Shareholders Meeting," Making Change at Walmart, 2018, http://changewalmart.org /whatiswalmarthiding/.

19. Craig McCrohon, "How to Hide in a Fish Bowl: Street-Smart Guide to Private Company Investor Disclosure," Burke, Warren, MacKay & Serritella, P.C., 12 Dec. 2012, http://www.burkelaw.com/pressroom-publications -Guide-to-Private-Company-Investor-Disclosure.html.

20. "AXA Stakeholder Advisory Panel," Profile and Key Figures, AXA, 2014, https://group.axa.com/en/about -us/stakeholder-advisory-panel.

21. "IESO Board Appoints New Stakeholder Advisory Committee and Technical Panel Members," IESO, 14 Dec. 2017, http://www.ieso.ca/en/sector-participants/ieso -news/2017/12/ieso-board-appoints-new-stakeholder -advisory-committee-and-technical-panel-members.

22. "The Essential Role of the Corporate Secretary to Enhance Board Sustainability Oversight: A Best Practices Guide," The United Nations Global Compact, Sept. 2016, https:// corostrandberg.com/wp-content/uploads/2016/11 /corporate-secretaries-guide-board-sustainability -governance.pdf.

23. Scott Berinato, Gretchen Gavett, and James Wheaton, "The Cost of Taking a Stand," *Harvard Business Review*, 23 Mar. 2018, https://hbr.org/2018/03/the-cost-of -taking-a-stand.

24. Susan McPherson, "8 Corporate Social Responsibility (CSR) Trends to Look For in 2018," *Forbes*, 12 Jan. 2018, https://www.forbes.com/sites/susanmcpherson /2018/01/12/8-corporate-social-responsibility-csr -trends-to-look-for-in-2018/#1ab049d040ce.

25. Excerpts from telephone interview with Pamela Coles, 7 Aug. 2018.

26. "The Essential Role of the Corporate Secretary to Enhance Board Sustainability Oversight: A Best Practices Guide." The United Nations Global Compact, Sept. 2016, https:// corostrandberg.com/wp-content/uploads/2016/11 /corporate-secretaries-guide-board-sustainability -governance.pdf.

27. Excerpts from telephone interview with Colin Low, 14 Aug. 2018.

CHAPTER 6

Directors and Personal Accountability

Boards that take competition seriously in the digital age will stay the most effective and vibrant. And board members who embrace the rate of change and make the effort to self-educate will be the most valuable.[1]

– Betsy Atkins

Value creation, just-in-time strategy, and achievement of ESG goals and activities all ultimately depend on optimal performance by individual directors. Meanwhile, there's been a massive expansion of responsibility and liability in corporate governance, putting individual board members under scrutiny and risk like never before.

In 2018, Facebook shareholder Jeremiah Hallisey sued a bevy of top executives: founder and CEO Mark Zuckerberg, COO Sheryl Sandberg, and board members Marc Andreessen, Peter Thiel, Reed Hastings, Erskine Bowles, Susan Desmond-Hellmann, and Jan Koum.[2] The charge: failing to prevent misappropriation of data by Cambridge Analytica and failing to inform affected Facebook users and the public markets.

This case represents just the tip of the iceberg. Directors and executives are facing shareholder lawsuits for losses stemming from crises like data breaches, sexual harassment and discrimination, poor incentive design, and beyond. Cases against companies from Home Depot to 21st Century Fox have accused directors and managers of failing to uphold their fiduciary duties of due care, loyalty, and good faith. For governance professionals, the pressure is on to protect their finances, careers, and reputations.

Just as boards as a whole have been increasingly pressed to do the right thing for the environment, the community, and for governance in general, directors as individuals face heightened pressure to provide better oversight, insight, and foresight.

But this is not your grandfather's era of fiduciary responsibility. Today's pace of change demands not only efficient governance professionals but high-performing ones as well, leaders who not only accelerate current processes but discover new ways of doing things.

Furthermore, in the current world of business volatility and digital transformation, the role of the governance professional has shifted from "trusted advisor" to "questioner-in-chief." It demands asking different questions and seeking different kinds of information. Often, there will be a greater expectation of transparency, especially from the media, the public, and activist shareholders.

To minimize the risk of disaster on their watch, board members need to hold themselves accountable like never before. How? Borrow a strategy from another sphere where high performance is imperative and continual improvement essential: professional football (or, in the United States, soccer). And we suggest focusing on the following three areas: playing by the rules, playing together as a team, and always bringing your "A game" to the table.

Playing by the Rules

Just as professional footballers are charged to follow the rules during their 90 minutes on the pitch, board members must obey all applicable laws and regulatory requirements. And the consequences of disobedience on a corporate board are much more than a red card or two minutes in the penalty box. A noncompliant governance professional risks regulatory actions, criminal investigations, heavy financial loss, reputational loss, and lengthy litigation.

Keeping up with legalities can be a challenge for a busy board member, especially in an evolving area like cybersecurity. Regulators worldwide are responding to data privacy concerns and cyber attacks of heightening scope and sophistication. In recent years, corporations (and their boards) have had to grapple not only with the European Union's GDPR but also cybersecurity regulations[3] in key centers of finance and commerce, such as the state of New York, China, and Singapore.

Today's board members need to have the latest, most relevant information. "Nevertheless, just 34 percent of boards on publicly traded companies received compliance and ethics training," Priya Cherian Huskins, partner/SVP and a director on the board of Woodruff Sawyer, a member of the board of directors of Realty Income Corporation, and a member of the advisory board of the Rock Center for Corporate Governance at Stanford University, wrote in a March 2018 article for Woodruff Sawyer,[4] "This is according to the '2017 Compliance Training and the Board Survey' by the Society of Corporate Compliance and Ethics, and the Health Care Compliance Association. Worse, when they did receive training, only 18 percent of board members were very satisfied with it."[5]

"You have so many atypical risks all hitting the tipping point in the past few years," said corporate director Nora Denzel. "You might not be able to predict the next disruptive risk that will manifest overnight; however, a more adaptive style of governance can help boards react and respond appropriately."[6]

With such an ongoing oversight role, the training burden doesn't lessen after the onboarding ends. Governance professionals already charged with the basic fundamental duties of strategic planning, monitoring, and oversight now have increasingly demanding regulations and expectations added to their plate. Because risk, compliance, and technology issues may complicate already long and complex board meeting agendas, many corporations delegate the bulk of this work to a committee.

Corporate director Laurie Yoler, who's served on the boards of Tesla, Church & Dwight, and Bose, presented the downsides of delegation – in this case, delegation of technology oversight. "How will the full board get comfortable with tech terms and issues if they are relegated to a single committee? The issues the company faces – like cyber – are so broad in their impact that you need to really determine what the full board should review vs. what the tech committee should handle."[7]

Ralph Loura, who's served as a technology executive with Rodan + Fields, Clorox, and HP, sees value in both perspectives. He has not yet been involved in a board with a dedicated technology committee, "but the need became apparent in several companies that I have been involved with." A tech committee can be a good step. However, care must be taken to roll vital issues like cybersecurity up to the board. "To effectively deal with technology oversight," Loura explained, "you need the whole board. It shouldn't be relegated to audit."[8]

Communication is key to making committees work. For example, compliance committees, like all committees, generally communicate with board members in the form of reports. Beyond this, there are no mandates regarding the information included in these reports. According to Deloitte, compliance committees face three major risks: not sharing enough information, not sharing the right information, and not sharing information in a timely manner.[9] As compliance committees perform these duties, board directors need to uphold responsibility on their side. They need to take the initiative to read compliance committee reports, ask questions, and respond in a measured, timely, and thoughtful fashion.

Technology solutions can help with the information-sharing aspect of these challenges. Structural and procedural safeguards can help directors avoid legal pitfalls. But tools and processes are only part of strengthening and maintaining accountability. Compliance must be prioritized by the board's culture, with systems for ensuring it is embedded into governance processes, controls, and operations.

A Global Perspective on Governance Best Practices[10]

Susan Forrester is a chairman and corporate director based in Australia, who serves on the boards of several public companies, including: director and chair of the Remuneration Committee, G8 Education Ltd.; chair and non-executive director of National Veterinary Care, Ltd.; director and chair of the Audit and Risk Committee, Over The Wire Ltd.; and director and chair of the People and Culture Committee, Xenith IP Ltd.

What have you been seeing in terms of accountability and risk in Australia?

There has been a large focus on this topic. The Australian Prudential Regulation Authority (APRA) recently released its final report into the governance, culture, and accountability within the Commonwealth Bank of Australia, Australia's largest bank. The report follows several damaging incidents and the high-profile AUSTRAC anti-money laundering proceedings. At the same time, there was a Royal Commission into Misconduct in the Banking, Superannuation, and Financial Services Industry.

APRA's overarching conclusion was that CBA's continued financial success had "dulled the senses of the institution" and led to a widespread sense of complacency in dealing with risk. The report was particularly critical of the CBA board's performance and the board's interaction with management.

Both reports revealed some earthshaking findings about boards not holding senior executives accountable.

Executives were receiving their full short- and long-term remuneration regardless of whether or not they were performing and upholding the appropriate risk and compliance procedures. Many of the banks looked like they were satisfying compliance procedures but were only doing a "tick the box" approach to compliance. Meanwhile, one financial institution was charging interest on accounts associated with individuals who were deceased, and charging inappropriate fees on funeral services to indigenous people. If you look at the banks and institutions that were involved in the financial crisis, either the boards didn't know what was going on or they knew and were complicit.

The findings were that too often financial institutions had pursued short-term profit at the expense of basic standards of honesty. How else can you explain charging continuing advice fees to the dead? Too often, selling became the sole focus of attention. Finance products and services multiplied, and the banks tried to maximize their share of the customer's wallet. From the executive suite to the front line, staff were measured and rewarded according to profit and sales. When misconduct was revealed, it either went unpunished, or the consequences did not reflect the seriousness of what had been done. The conduct regulator, ASIC, rarely went to court to seek punishment for misconduct. The prudential regulator, APRA, never went to court. When misconduct was revealed, little happened beyond an apology from the entity, a drawn-out remediation program, or an infringement notice.

What remedies have been proposed to this situation?

Although some of the remedies relate to regulated financial institutions, many of the recommendations have broader relevance because they focus on board performance and approach to organizational culture and risk.

(continued)

Australian directors should be aware of the comments and recommendations made by APRA and need to consider how their internal processes match up to what APRA has recommended.

Some of the key governance themes underpinning APRA's recommendations are:

- Strengthening accountability structures between the board, audit and risk committee, and executive and senior leadership teams.

- An expectation that the board will assess and ensure that senior executive remuneration outcomes reflect individual and collective accountability for material adverse risk management and compliance outcomes.

The commission wants to see a renewed focus on the role and responsibility of the board and executive and senior leadership teams for monitoring and ensuring the escalation of significant risk issues, including regulatory, audit, and other financial and operating risks. This will require a substantial upgrading of the authority, status, and capability of a board's compliance functions and operational risk functions.

Boards will be required to put more emphasis on achieving good organizational culture that starts at the top – to be reinforced and consistently applied by all leaders.

Australian law already requires financial institutions to "do all things necessary to ensure" that the services they are licensed to provide are provided "efficiently, honestly and fairly." The conduct condemned by the regulators was contrary to law. Passing new laws to say, again, "Do not do that," would add an extra layer of legal complexity to an already complex regulatory regime. What does that gain? Should the existing law be administered or enforced differently?

Unfortunately, many boards will focus on complying with checklists and feel they have satisfied their new level of accountability. In doing so, they miss the importance of demanding transparency and accountability from each director. Rather than focus on a checklist, directors should spend time discussing how they can improve their own performance in-line with the new recommendations. Change needs to be more holistic, more comprehensive, with increased accountability. There needs to be a focus on candor, rather than groupthink.

Is good governance more cultural or structural?

We all know that boards need to have disciplined accountability structures, and compliance processes can always be tightened up. But if we just review structure, and not culture, we're only seeing half of the problem. It reminds me of the [Peter Drucker] saying "Culture eats strategy for breakfast!" We need to pay attention to how the board works with management to acquit their role, how they develop trust, and how they support one another.

You earn trust through regular interactions, through phone calls and discussions. You earn it through how you handle difficult situations, like letting a CEO go. Or having a tough discussion with shareholders on why you missed your numbers last quarter.

Look at how you're developing trust with your CEO. Are you receiving timely, high-quality information? If board members don't feel they have the information to make good decisions, there's an erosion of trust. Have regular check-ins on how the board is doing beyond a detailed checklist review once a year.

A board, like other governing bodies like a parliament or the United Nations, is challenged to become a high-performing team even though they only meet a

(continued)

handful of times per year. It's a social system and it isn't going to get there in terms of effectiveness just because it's well-structured. There needs to be trust, respect, and a strong bond.

What practical steps can boards take to have these discussions?

Rather than slavishly following a monthly board agenda, a practical option is to tailor the agenda for five or so critical issues that need to get discussed. This way, you can have time for robust discussion of the issues that really need to be addressed. Meanwhile, shorter, more dynamic discussion sessions with management should occur to review what's happening with the strategy. And these should occur on a fairly real-time basis, rather than the typical twice-a-year review.

Are you seeing technology change the way boards work?

I'm surprised by how many directors still use paper. When they show up to meetings with books at 1,000 pages and they can't toggle back-and-forth quickly enough, it's a real constraint. We expect our management teams to be digitally savvy, and we should expect the same from our directors.

I'd like to see directors being trained in the use of video and telephone conferencing. Often, when quick decisions are required, such technology is necessary, but its effectiveness is impeded by directors who are not competent or confident enough to use it.

Playing Well Together

Today more than ever, the popular saying "there is no 'I' in team" holds true. Governance professionals must put the interests of the board and the corporation above their own – including keeping confidentiality sacred, speaking with one voice outside of the boardroom, and avoiding conflicts of interest.

In 2017–2018, Papa John's Pizza[11] provided a cautionary tale of what happens when leadership doesn't play well together. Company founder and board chairman John Schnatter reportedly began to undermine a new CEO when marketing campaigns didn't feature him. Then, Schnatter defied board instructions by making unscripted comments blaming the NFL and its National Anthem controversy for poor pizza sales. A special committee of the board accused Schnatter of "promoting his self-interest at the expense of all others in an attempt to regain control" of the company. When the board pressed Schnatter to meet with them, he offered his attendance on one condition: that the company cancel an annual franchise meeting. (His request was denied.)

Boards can't prevent all forms of infighting and discord; however, they can put structures and processes in place for managing the risk and impact. They can support directors with policies that keep up with changing times on matters like whistle-blowing, noncompliance reporting, and conflicts of interest.

For instance, evolving business models spurred by digital transformation are making conflicts of interest more challenging to detect and enforce. Consider how a change in strategic focus can transform the competitive landscape. The move from DVDs to streaming TV programs put Netflix in direct competition with broadcast networks. And when Amazon launched its own private-label clothing brands, it added women's apparel companies to its roster of competitors. Boards should regularly review board policies against these developments and revisit their conflicts of interest questionnaires accordingly.

Meanwhile, governance professionals need to keep traditional conflict of interest triggers on their radar. Outsized compensation and personal agendas are still risks for directors acting in their own interests, rather than that of the board – and can be particularly destructive to board members' team dynamics.[12] Boards should be structured to support good director behavior, with strong internal controls, checks and balances, and reporting systems that are frequently monitored.

A Next-Gen Take on Culture, Cultivation, and Personal Accountability[13]

Priya Cherian Huskins is a partner/SVP and a director serving on the board of Woodruff Sawyer, a member of the board of directors of Realty Income Corporation, and a member of the Advisory Board of the Rock Center for Corporate Governance at Stanford University.

How do you create a healthy boardroom culture – one where personal accountability is expected by all directors?

You have to allow time for dialogue and the exchange of information. When you're onboarding people, you can help them understand what the norms and expectations are for their behavior by being explicit – for example, clarifying that they are expected to come to meetings prepared. This clarification exercise can serve as a reminder to the entire board of what the expectations are.

As a matter of good governance, I also try to be very clear in my mind about what is management's job versus what is the board's job. Having said that, there are times when the board, despite some discomfort it may feel, will need to step into what feels like a more hands-on role, for example, when a board has to deal with a #MeToo scandal. At a moment like this, it's helpful to remember that management gets its authority through delegation by the board; in some extraordinary situations, directors may have to modify or even suspend this delegation for the good of the shareholders they serve.

A systematic board refreshment process is another way to remind the board about its job and is a natural way to evaluate how a board is functioning. Being systematic about board refreshment also causes good board members to maintain a learner's mind-set, something that helps stave off the unfortunate, and dangerous, circumstance of becoming passive. Because we live in a time of rapid change, it's important to have people on the board who are willing to gather new information and even change their minds based on this new information. This might be in contrast with some directors who rely entirely and exclusively on their past experience. It's a poor outcome for shareholders if directors only discuss issues and make decisions based on experiences and circumstances that may no longer be relevant today.

What works best in recruiting and cultivating next-gen directors?

The most successful cultivation of next-gen leadership happens when the board takes on the responsibility to find the best fit, when a board realizes this effort isn't "one and done," and when a board allocates enough time and effort to integrate the new board member into the culture of the board.

When it comes to recruiting, the robust electronic social platforms that exist today give us an unprecedented level of visibility into an individual's work history and, in some cases, thought processes. This can be a great thing because we can use these social networks to discover and get to know people in ways that differ from the old recruitment model

(continued)

of "who do I know personally," which was more limited. One of the roles tech plays with boards today is to vastly expand our reach when it comes to discovering talent.

When it comes to integrating a new member onto the board, and even though a lot of new directors can figure things out on their own, it works best when the board is committed to making the process a smooth one. Deliberate actions like inviting a new board member out to breakfast before or after a meeting – things we would naturally do when we want a team member to be integrated well – can make a big difference.

Onboarding a next-gen board member doesn't require anything so different from onboarding any other new director. When a board makes assumptions about veteran or next-gen board members, a board might run into challenges if these assumptions turn out to be wrong. In this way, everyone benefits from a thoughtful and robust onboarding process.

What prevents more next-gen leaders from joining corporate boards?

Some boards are concerned that a next-gen leader just doesn't have enough business experience or "seasoning" to be a contributor. That may well be true in some circumstances, which is why the search process has to be robust. It's worth noting that age is not always a good proxy for business acumen. There are important competencies, for example an understanding of social media and technology disruption, where next-gen leaders can shine. Also, some boards are also concerned about a next-gen leader having enough time and control over his or her schedule to engage thoughtfully. This concern underscores why it's so important to talk to that individual about his or her particular circumstances and constraints, or lack thereof.

It would be a shame to lose a good candidate due to an assumption about schedule inflexibility that may not turn out to be true.

How much do directors need to know to be effective?

This is a tough question because it's so company-specific. It's also a very important question, and it ties directly to personal accountability. Independent directors need to inform themselves well enough to make independent judgments about the issues placed in front of them. When analyzing an issue and thinking about the risks and opportunities of a particular situation, effective directors will be able to reflect thoughtfully on whether or not their board needs more information, should form a working group, or should take a particular issue to a pre-existing committee. They will also bring new things they have learned into the boardroom before a company is in a critical situation. Going back to the "learner's mind-set," the best directors tend to be the most widely read in multiple disciplines. For example, if all you ever read are financial reports and news, you may miss something important that could impact your company when it comes to a changing demographic landscape or other competitive threats.

Preparation: Bringing Your "A" Game to the Table

I've been talking to boards since I graduated from college with a degree in tech. They tell me they struggle with staying current on tech trends, and I try to point out that even though I don't have a law degree or accounting degree, I manage to review legal and financial risk.

– Laurie Yoler

On the field and in the boardroom, performance is about strengthening your ability to do what your teammates and team are relying on you to do. The first step involves putting in the time, just as a professional footballer does for practice and conditioning. The second step involves upping your game. Every worker in today's transforming business climate knows the challenge of exponentially increasing responsibilities, and governance professionals are no different. Quarterly meetings have expanded to six to eight meetings a year. Roles have expanded to include communicating directly with employees, customers, and investors. And there's little forgiveness or sympathy for the ill-prepared.

Directors can start by "playing activist investor on themselves," quizzing themselves on their knowledge of critical policies in key areas: codes of conduct, conflicts of interest, securities trading, compensation and reimbursement, nominations, diversity, whistleblowers, and remuneration.

As issues shift and grow more complex, it's important to enforce a strict focus on what's oversight/non-executive (what the board should focus on) and what's something management/the executive team should be handling, advised Rolls-Royce company secretary Pamela Coles. "Our employee champion comes across things that are executive rather than non-executive in nature and takes these things to management."

"With dashboards, the KPIs need to fit the strategy," she continued. "Furthermore, you can look at scorecards, but things are not going to stand still. Life isn't like that. You're going to need to transform and reinvent yourself."

> ## Checklist: Learning Life Hacks for Governance Professionals
>
> Corporate Director Laurie Yoler provides tips on how directors can stay up to speed on our changing world:
>
> * Get weekly updates on tech and other subjects from news sources like NACD and *The Wall Street Journal.*
> * Listen to podcasts.
> * Watch TED Talks.
> * Seek out university and community lectures on timely issues.
> * Attend conferences on subjects other than governance.
> * Read topical books like *Bad Blood*, John Carreyrou's exposé on the downfall of medical startup Theranos.
> * Invite outside experts to meet and speak to your board.
> * And, when in doubt, simply speak up and ask questions.

Technology can help. Moving certain director functions online can increase transparency, accessibility, accountability, and efficiency. Consider the infamous, time-consuming, and very much required directors and officers (D&O) questionnaire. From the perspective of a board director or officer, a paper D&O questionnaire, often 30 to 80 pages long, is a task ripe for procrastination and cutting corners, even for the most dedicated board member.[14] Distributing and submitting such a form securely online and recycling basic information (like contact details from previous online form submissions) can increase the speed and likelihood of a response and the quality of the answers.

And this is just one example of where we see technology emerging to support governance professionals in their quest for greater personal accountability. For collaboration, boards have been borrowing from industries like law to implement tools like virtual data rooms. Meanwhile, voting capabilities, legal documents, surveys, and questionnaires have all been moving in a digital direction for quite some time, and digital meeting support has been around for more than a decade.[15]

Corporations, including the health technology firm Medtronic, have been reporting better meeting preparation and more time for collaboration through the use of an online board portal. The multiboard entity Heineken Pensions in the UK uses such a tool not only for meeting preparation[16] – making reports available days before quarterly meetings, along with papers from previous meetings – but also for professional development. Consider the possibilities for new directors, who can absorb the context of the board's work, the corporation's history, and major obstacles and milestones from past boards, on the go from a secure tablet or smartphone. Then consider the potential for these directors to make prescient and valuable contributions, armed with such rich and timely information.

Ultimately, digital tools will have to do more than speed up current processes, however. They will need to empower the new types of inquiry and information governance professionals will be employing in their role as skilled questioners. In this evolution, we see today's digital tools evolving into digital dashboards and ecosystems. Imagine governance support as a combination of an Alexa or Echo personal assistant; an easily searchable Google Docs; Google itself for accessing real-time, relevant archives powered by machine learning; and the best of all social media platforms. With only a glance at their phones, tablets, or whatever device the future holds, directors will be able to get actionable information about financial reports, strategic plans, operations, risk management, and more. Here AI is a trend to watch, not only for how it's shaping the competitive landscape, but also for its potential to deliver timely, personalized information for board-level decision making.

Nelson Chan, board chair with Adesto Technologies and board member for Deckers Outdoor Corp., describes the benefits of – and the need for – this future digital tool. "If I had one location, one source of information, that could keep me current – curated for me, by industry, by role, by areas of interest – it would be so helpful. Right now, there are so many places you can go, and I have to go seek it out."[17]

This exciting future, however, does not solve the challenges of today. And to reference back to our soccer analogy, tools and tactics are only part of helping directors become more personally accountable in challenging times. Teamwork and interpersonal dynamics are essential as well.

On a truly effective board, directors trust each other, so they're able to share difficult information. They all have access to the same comprehensive stores of data, so they're able to discuss issues from the same page. And because debate is the norm, they're able to act as questioners open to new ways of doing things rather than as rubber-stampers of the status quo.

Beyond compliance checklists, bylaws, disclosure forms, and other director requirements, true fiduciary responsibility lies in being able to add value in the most efficient, effective way possible. Making a board and corporation the best they can be in response to evolving circumstances is at the heart of personal accountability for the next generation of governance professionals.

Key Takeaways on Directors' Personal Accountability

- **Put in the time.** It's up to you to be conversant with your board's policies and bylaws and the laws and regulations governing your industry.
- **Prioritize compliance.** Create systems to ensure it's embedded into all governance processes, controls, and operations.
- **Communicate.** Share information in a timely manner with fellow board members, committees, and management, and leverage the tools and technologies available in the marketplace for doing so securely and efficiently. And don't be afraid to ask candid questions.
- **Put the interests of the board and the corporation above your own.** Keep confidentiality sacred, speak with one voice outside the boardroom, and avoid conflicts of interest.

Notes

1. Excerpt from telephone interview with Betsy Atkins, 21 Aug. 2018.
2. Natasha Lomas, "Facebook Hit with Shareholder Lawsuits over Data Misuse Crisis," *TechCrunch*, 23 Mar. 2018, https://techcrunch.com/2018/03/23/facebook-hit-with-shareholder-lawsuits-over-data-misuse-crisis/.
3. Juliette Rizkallah, "The Cybersecurity Regulatory Crackdown," *Forbes*, 25 Aug. 2017, https://www.forbes.com/sites/forbestechcouncil/2017/08/25/the-cybersecurity-regulatory-crackdown/#30bc75454573.
4. Priya Cherian Huskins, "Keeping in Compliance and Out of Trouble with the DOJ: The Benefits of Board Education Training,". Woodruff Sawyer, 28 Mar. 2018, https://woodruffsawyer.com/do-notebook/board-education-training-compliance-doj/.

5. Excerpt from telephone interview with Priya Cherian Huskins, 14 Aug. 2018.
6. Excerpts from telephone interview with Nora Denzel, 6 Sept. 2018.
7. Excerpt from telephone interview with Laurie Yoler, 2 Aug. 2018.
8. Excerpts from telephone interview with Ralph Loura, 23 July 2018.
9. Maureen Bujno, "Why Improving Board Communication Is Time Well Spent," CFO Insights, Deloitte, 2013, https://www2.deloitte.com/us/en/pages/finance /articles/cfo-insights-board-communication-director -risk-management.html.
10. Excerpts from telephone interview with Susan Forrester, 20 Aug. 2018.
11. Chris Morris, "Papa John's Board Rips Into Papa John in New Open Letter," *Fortune*, 30 Aug. 2018, http://www .fortune.com/2018/08/30/papa-johns-board-open-letter -john-schnatter.
12. Jeffrey A. Sonnenfeld, "What Makes Great Boards Great," *Harvard Business Review*, Sept. 2002, https://hbr .org/2002/09/what-makes-great-boards-great.
13. Excerpts from telephone interview with Priya Cherian Huskins, 14 Aug. 2018.
14. Nicholas J. Price, "Best Practices for Director & Officer (D&O) Questionnaires | Diligent," Diligent Corporation, 30 May 2018, https://diligent.com/blog/best-practices -for-do-questionnaires.
15. "Case Study: Diligent Moves Medtronic's Board Collaboration Forward," Diligent Corporation, 2018, https://diligent.com/resources/diligent-moves -medtronics-board-collaboration-forward.
16. "Case Study: Heineken Pensions and Diligent Boards: Brewing Better Decision Making," Diligent Corporation, 2018, https://diligent.com/resources/heineken-pensions -and-diligent-boards-brewing-better-decision-making.
17. Excerpt from telephone interview with Nelson Chan, 3 Aug. 2018.

PART 2

Framework for Modern Governance

CHAPTER 7

Board Behavioral Profiles: A Governance Roadmap for the Digital Age

Unlike many other roles within the company, the governance role rarely comes with a clear roadmap. For many positions in a company, extensive training, support, and written documentation are provided on the norms, procedures, and standards for each area of responsibility. Directors, meanwhile, are expected to join a board fully prepared to navigate a wide variety of sensitive, complex, and challenging issues with minimal guidance. Many issues cannot be discussed outside the confines of the boardroom, let alone be documented in writing, which means that detailed procedural manuals, training, and ongoing operational support for the governance role are rather rare.

Boards are increasingly expected to function as high-performing teams. Yet, the nature of board work is such that directors meet only a handful of times throughout the year, spend much of their time in meetings passively listening to presentations, and are actively discouraged from having sidebar conversations or contacting employees directly to seek answers to questions. The likelihood that any group of individuals could become a high-performing team under these conditions is low indeed.

Meanwhile, technology serves as both a catalyst and a backdrop to all of the changes taking place in corporate governance. Directors are feeling increasing pressure to become tech-savvy – not only from the standpoint of the technology tools they use, but in terms of their ability to spot potential areas of risk facing their organizations and to be eager proponents of new opportunities fueled by technology.

Even for those who have been in their roles for years, governance is a tough job with little to no support beyond the boardroom. While some in the governance role successfully tap into peer networks – either by creating relationships themselves or by joining professional associations that assure discussions remain confidential – most are left to figure everything out on their own. It's not surprising that many directors and governance professionals alike wonder, "Am I the only one who's experienced something like this?" The answer is a resounding "No."

Suggested Framework for Board Behaviors

Our framework identifies four distinct Board Behavioral Profiles (see Table 7.1). The goal is to help those in governance roles identify the behavioral characteristics of their board and to suggest pathways for

Table 7.1 Governance in the Digital Age: Board Behavioral Profiles

	Foundational Board	Structural Board	Catalyst Board	Futuristic Board
Description and focus	• Meeting basic requirements and driving growth. • Focus: **growth**	• Board serves as watchdog. • Focus: **governance & oversight**	Board drives results in a "turnaround" capacity. Focus: **transformation**	Board is a strategic resource for long-term performance. Focus: **legacy**
Common traits	• Board is small (< 5), with few independent directors. • Informal processes.	• Board grows in size. • More independent directors. • Processes formalized. • Governance staffing.	• Directors drive change. • Separate CEO and board chair. • Focus on outcomes drives adoption of new processes.	• Independent directors. • Succession and board resilience are top of mind. • Innovative board processes.
Board meetings and processes	• Efficient, but informal. • Few meetings and committees. • Minimal documentation. • No board support staff.	• Meetings focus on reporting and discussion of results. • Extensive board materials. • Processes are better defined.	• Focus on discussion of adaptation, positive change. • Increased board education and committee engagement.	• Directors drive the agenda. • Meetings are strategic discussions. • Directors create broad peer networks.

(continued)

125

Table 7.1 Governance in the Digital Age: Board Behavioral Profiles

	Foundational Board	Structural Board	Catalyst Board	Futuristic Board
Tech approach and tools in use	Tech tools don't play a prominent role in the board's work – email and basic online repositories for documents might be in use.	The board begins to use online tools to facilitate meetings and automate compliance requirements, such as online resolutions and voting, minutes, and board evaluations.	Catalyst Boards use online tools to facilitate meetings, track progress, and increase director collaboration – such as agenda building, board peer evaluations, secure messaging, and online board education.	In addition to online meeting management, compliance and collaboration tools, Futuristic Boards want real-time content: dashboards and scorecards on areas of compliance, risk, and board effectiveness.
Outcomes	Board takes its lead from management, but also probes management for areas of untapped potential.	Board understands its role is to ask better questions; possible answers are still supplied by management.	Board acknowledges its role in company transformation, and becomes hungry for better data, analyses, insights, and education.	Board understands its role as a strategic asset for long-term value. Directors adopt a "coaching role" with the CEO.
Key drivers to change profile	As directors gain knowledge and experience in governance, they see a need to exert more direct oversight and develop more formal governance practices.	Directors feel they have at least a basic handle on compliance, and seek ways to work more collaboratively.	Directors foster strategic relationships with executive team; directors seek better insights, and begin to think about legacy.	Directors understand their strategic role, and can self-identify when it's time for them to step aside and make room for fresh perspectives.

directors to follow for consciously altering their board's approach to governance. These Board Behavioral Profiles describe the four ways boards govern in the digital age: the primary focuses, common traits, approaches to board meetings and governance processes, use of governance technology tools, expected outcomes, and key drivers to change.

We derived these profiles through a combination of interviews with directors, research on current governance practices and trends, and observation from our direct work with corporate leaders. We found in our conversations with directors that their boards' Behavioral Profiles ebb and flow on a spectrum based on circumstance and business need. Boards do not necessarily follow a linear path from left to right through the four profiles, and sometimes adopt aspects of multiple profiles as situations evolve. For example, directors reported their boards might adopt a completely different profile temporarily in times of crisis: a Foundational Board might find itself adopting the behaviors and norms of Structural Boards, should the organization be rocked by a scandal implicating its top leaders. Likewise, directors of Catalyst Boards could find themselves leaning into the Futuristic Board profile when investors press them to focus more on innovation, long-term value creation, leadership succession, and sustainability.

We hope that directors find utility in this framework as a roadmap and predictive tool, and that it helps directors identify what boards might experience and suggest how they might approach making changes as desired.

The Foundational Board

Foundational Board: Description and Focus

Foundational Boards are most commonly found in newer organizations (those that have been in existence for less than 10 years), but can be present in long-lived organizations as well. While forming a board might occur at the moment of birth for many enterprises, not all organizations are required to form a board at the outset.[1] Regardless of the age of the organization, the hallmarks of Foundational Boards are their basic structures and focus on driving growth. The Foundational Board often doesn't have a strong identity as a separate and independent governing body, but rather serves as an extension of the executive team.

Any governance structures and processes usually exist only to comply with external regulation or internal pressure. In this sense, efficiency is usually the primary goal for Foundational Board meetings. There are fewer formal governance processes for this board profile, and it's not uncommon for these boards to skip some of the basic meeting procedures, such as making and seconding motions, tallying formal votes, and formally approving of minutes. It is rare to find many committees on Foundational Boards – and rarer still to find written documentation on board operational procedures – such as one would find in a board handbook or board manual – for Foundational Boards.

That said, when Foundational Boards meet, their focus is usually on organizational growth and development. Foundational Boards often are hands-on in their approach to overseeing the executive management team. In some cases, such as in many private family-owned enterprises, the board is mostly comprised of senior executives. Because of these trends, Foundational Boards can struggle to keep the governance role separate from the management role and can be accused of micromanaging the executive team.

One of my boards falls into the Foundational Board profile, which is a fundamental profile for any public company focused on growth, operating efficiently, and making an impact. If you're a public company in today's context, it's all about growth – to create an impact. The board has to be efficient – you just have a few meetings, and focus on growth.[2]

– Colin Low, chairman of the board of directors of Singapore Investment Development Corporation (SIDC)

Common Traits of Foundational Boards

Foundational Boards are typically comprised of a small group of insiders. Whether they be executives of the company or very close associates – the directors are likely to be only those who have strong interests in the success of the enterprise. It's common for Foundational Boards to have fewer than five members, most of whom are executives of the company.[3] For this board profile, board diversity is rarely a strong area of focus. Rather, Foundational Board membership is usually restricted to a small trusted group of insiders who know one another well enough to make consensus relatively easy to reach. Indeed, consensus is often considered the only acceptable way to make decisions, with any strong dissent on an issue halting discussion in its tracks.

Foundational Boards also take a more passive approach to the risk-oversight role. Because the board tends to have few committees and formal processes, areas of risk might only be discussed as the need arises – either because an incident has occurred (such as a cyber breach), or because of a regulatory requirement. Foundational Boards don't tend to proactively seek out areas of potential risk or a strategic approach to their oversight role.

Foundational Board Meetings and Processes

Foundational Boards place a high value on efficiency. Board meetings tend to be kept brief, with reviewing financial performance as the primary focus. The bulk of directors' time in board meetings is spent listening to reports from management and asking clarifying questions focused on growth.

I sit on an advisory board of a family-run business – a Foundational Board. For this board, it would be absolutely wrong that they move to the right side of the spectrum. The CEO, who is the founder and 90-plus percentage majority owner, wouldn't want this. She's got a great board of people with diverse and relevant backgrounds, and she pulls us together three or four times a year with specific questions and her agenda. In the course of that efficient and informal procedure, we're sometimes very "catalytic" – we ask the CEO questions like, "Have you thought about this?" But our meetings are informal and efficient.[4]

– Jan Babiak, director on the boards of directors of Walgreens Boots Alliance, Euromoney Institutional Investor, and Bank of Montreal

---

Foundational Boards usually don't have governance-specific staffing. Corporate secretarial duties are usually performed by one of the senior executives attending board meetings, such as the CFO or the COO. Directors might be asked to debate the merits of different strategic approaches and to provide their unique perspectives, but most of these discussions are held first by the management team before the board is asked to weigh in. The board might then be asked to simply approve the plan and its related financial investments. Because of this dynamic, when directors seek to initiate discussion of new ideas or different strategic approaches, they might be accused of micromanagement or of straying outside the governance role.

Given the nature of Foundational Board work, board meeting agendas tend to be kept brief and meeting materials fairly lean, focused mostly on financials and management reports. Indeed, there might only be a few formal governance processes in place or few (or no) committees in place, with all functions – such as nominations, governance oversight, financial oversight, and so forth – being handled by the full board as a "committee of the whole." Depending on the type of organization, an audit committee might exist to fulfill the requirement for independent audits; but this group might meet only once or a handful of times each year and focus its energy solely on ensuring an independent financial audit takes place. Rarely are the audit committees of Foundational Boards given a mandate to proactively identify, or create plans to address, areas of risk for the organization.

Additionally, Foundational Boards might take a somewhat passive approach to risk oversight. There are unlikely to be lengthy conversations at the board table about areas of risk unless and until a crisis or threat to the organization is apparent. Even then, the board might continue to take a more passive approach to risk oversight, seeing its role more as taking direction from, and providing support to, the management team as the organization navigates through the crisis rather than assigning directors specific lead roles in crisis response.

Tech and Tools in Use by Foundational Boards

For this board profile, there might not be much technology in place to facilitate or augment governance processes. Since Foundational Boards usually have only the most basic governance structures and mostly informal governance processes, technology is not perceived as a critical need by these boards. One barrier to leveraging technology tools is a lack of governance-specific staff to oversee implementation and provide ongoing support to ensure the tools and the information they contain is kept current. That said, with efficiency and growth as primary concerns, this board might use video conferencing tools, email, and a basic online repository of financial reports to help ensure that directors have convenient access to meetings, including remote attendance as needed.

Outcomes for Foundational Boards

Foundational Boards often take their lead from senior management – especially as many of the directors are also senior executives of the organization. Essentially, when the organization is growing, the board "does as directed" with little dissent or challenge posed by directors. When growth stalls or other signs of trouble appear, the board might become actively engaged in determining and directing the organization's strategy. This often poses challenges to the senior management team, who may chafe against this hands-on approach.

Foundational Boards' Key Drivers to Change

As directors gain knowledge and experience in governance, they begin to perceive a need for more formal governance practices. In some cases, a change of executive leadership produces a strong incentive for the board to increase its level of governance oversight. As the organization evolves, the board's concern about its level of compliance with applicable laws, regulations, and best practices grows. Directors begin to feel that providing more oversight could yield better results – particularly as those results relate to the quality of the chief executive's performance and the need for directors to give that individual higher-level support and guidance (without stepping on the CEO's toes). These concerns about compliance and director involvement can propel the board to adopt a different Board Behavioral Profile.

Foundational Boards that are on the cusp of changing their Board Behavioral Profile might ask themselves:

- Does our board composition reflect the diversity of skillsets and perspectives we need in order to support our growth objectives?
- Do we have adequate governance structures and processes in place to allow governance to function smoothly, even if we experience a rapid turnover in leadership?
- Are we providing adequate risk oversight?

The Structural Board

Structural Board: Description and Focus

Every board, regardless of its profile, has oversight as one of its primary responsibilities; in fact, many would argue that oversight is the most important function of any board.[5] What sets apart the profile of Structural Boards is their focus on oversight to the exclusion of nearly everything else. Structural Boards view their primary role as that of being the checks and balances for the senior management team – and, in particular, for the chief executive.

Structural Boards are focused on legal compliance with regulations, adherence to bylaws and precedent, and serving as the watchdog for the potential abuses that come with executive power. Depending on the organization's country of origin, the directors of Structural Boards might have a personal financial stake in the company as shareholders or investors. Even when personal financial interests are discouraged or highly regulated—as is the case for many companies in the EU,[6] these directors still view their role as representing the interests of shareholders and investors. It's not uncommon for the Structural Board to seek out new director candidates who have legal and/or compliance expertise. It's also typical for the company secretary and/or general counsel of the organization to start to play an expanded role in directly managing the board's work: helping prepare reports and documents for board meetings, identifying discussion topics the board should include on its schedule, and providing feedback on compliance issues for the board's consideration.

Common Traits of Structural Boards

With the increased focus on oversight comes increased attention to formal governance processes. Structural Boards usually have a more detailed set of governance guidelines that expand upon the basic foundation created by the bylaws and codified in a board handbook or other written manual outlining expectations, procedures, and protocols for the board to follow. Structural Boards typically have a few standing committees: an independent audit committee that takes on a more powerful and pivotal role in carrying out the oversight role for the organization; a nominating/governance committee focused on identifying prospective directors as needed; and an executive compensation or remuneration committee, focused on executive compensation and performance review.

As part of the development of more formal governance processes, the Structural Board often will conduct a review of the existing bylaws and board policies, and establish more formal procedures for board meetings. It's common to see Structural Boards seeking better governance staffing – encouraging the chief executive to hire or appoint a company secretary or other governance-support professional tasked with ensuring that board meetings proceed according to policy and that compliance requirements are being met.

While Structural Boards can vary, generally speaking, they tend to be larger than Foundational Boards and, depending on the organization's country of origin, they also tend to have more non-executive/independent directors. Where Foundational Boards value having a small group of "insiders," Structural Boards begin to see advantages in having both a larger group of directors as well as more independent voices at the board table. The push for more independent directors is often an attempt by Structural Boards to ensure better compliance, reduce potential conflicts of interest, and provide stronger checks and balances for the senior management team.

Structural Board Meetings and Processes

Because Structural Boards place such a high value on regulatory and legal compliance, their meetings tend to last longer, with a good portion of directors' time spent reviewing reports, discussing results, and reviewing any related risks facing the organization. In board meetings, directors can often be found asking detailed (and sometimes pointed) questions of the senior management team about whether or not a particular program or strategy will be in compliance with regulatory and legal requirements, and whether or not the plan invites undue risk.

The Structural Board highly values the involvement of legal counsel and/or other compliance-focused staff in board meetings on a regular basis. Many Structural Boards will recommend that the chief executive hire or appoint a governance professional to help ensure all the work is getting done on time. The person in this role might be a support member of the chief executive's staff, or a member of the legal staff, and/or a Company Secretary might be hired with support of the board as the new hire's primary job function.

Given the expanding view Structural Boards have of governance work, their board meeting agendas tend to be more extensive than those of Foundational Boards. Structural Board directors spend more time debating strategic approaches from the perspective of how those approaches will impact the organization from a legal, compliance, and risk-mitigation perspective. This is not to say that Structural Boards have no concern about growth or organizational performance; on the contrary, Structural Boards see oversight as a primary means to ensuring strong results. It's not uncommon for Structural Board meetings to spend time in board and committee meetings discussing the merits of specific board policies, with careful attention paid to the exact phrasing.

The audit committees of Structural Boards also tend to have an expanded risk oversight and mitigation role – for example, ensuring compliance with the latest data privacy laws and cybersecurity regulations, and meeting as frequently (or even more frequently) than the full board. Not surprisingly, Structural Boards take an active approach to risk oversight, including creating detailed crisis-response plans that involve the board in tangible ways.

Tech and Tools in Use by Structural Boards

Structural Boards commonly begin to seek out better tools and resources as their compliance work expands. As board meetings and related papers become more extensive, and the quantity of governance documentation grows, the board's need for better ways to organize, search, and access this information becomes more acute. Structural Boards often ask their key governance-support professional or company secretary to find solutions that will allow the board to have convenient, secure, and searchable access to the growing body of board documents.

Additionally, Structural Boards might also perceive the need for tools that help them complete certain compliance tasks, such as: collecting conflict-of-interest forms, directors and officers questionnaires, or other re-quired disclosures; completing board self-assessments; gaining board approvals on resolutions; and gather-ing directors' signatures on newly approved policies. It's not uncommon for Structural Boards to seek out software and other resources that can not only au-tomate some of the compliance work, but can also provide audit trails that help confirm the board's com-pliance with various requirements from regulators and legislatures.

Outcomes for Structural Boards

Whereas Foundational Boards often take their lead from senior management, only dissenting when growth is in question, Structural Boards see their role more as demanding answers from senior management and en-suring that the organization is being run legally and ethically. They understand that their job is to ask more (and better) questions – to be curious, even suspicious. This is particularly true when a board adopts the Struc-tural Board profile on the heels of a major legal or ethi-cal crisis for the organization.

While this increased attention from the board can certainly help the organization navigate areas of risk, the burden of proof still resides squarely with the sen-ior management team. Directors might request the staff to provide multiple options for how to proceed on an issue or seek clarification and additional detail to ensure they are doing an adequate job of oversight. The outcome is that the amount of material the board must review grows substantially, and the amount of time directors and executives spend preparing for board meetings likewise expands.

Structural Boards' Key Drivers to Change

As board processes become more formalized and directors spend more time reviewing detailed information, directors begin to feel that they might be losing the forest for the trees – that by reviewing so much detail, they might miss potential areas of risk or opportunity that could help propel transformation.

Eventually, Structural Boards begin to crave better analyses. They begin asking for more executive summaries with key insights from the executive team as a preface to detailed reports. In part, this is driven by directors' realization that focusing only on compliance and oversight won't lead to dynamic change – that there might need to be something more directors will do to fuel growth and value creation. In some cases, the timing of this growing desire to shift focus from compliance to transformation coincides with the strengthening of an organization that has successfully survived a legal or ethical crisis, or has identified new opportunities fueled by technological innovation. For example, Structural Boards often receive pressure from investors to focus less of their time on purely compliance-related issues, and to pay more attention to strategy development and innovation. These external pressures, combined with the board's internal desire to "know and do more," can lead to changes in the board's profile.

This board [I'm on] that challenges itself to discern strategy started as a Structural Board – focused on governance and oversight. Then we had a "near death" experience. There were competitive moves we didn't anticipate, and the industry has a long lead time of two to three years. We needed a cash infusion, and everything was about staying alive, so we didn't have the luxury of focusing on governance. We had to pare it back to the basics. We went back to the Foundational [Board] level and focused on growth and turnaround. Now we have earnings, and as a board, we're looking out and beyond. The board's profile has to fit the purpose. You might know how to eat right, drink water, exercise ... but if you suddenly find yourself on a desert island, you have to change how you behave. You can't just keep going the same way as before.[7]

– Nora Denzel, director of the
boards of directors of Advanced Micro
Devices (AMD), Ericsson, and Talend SA

Once directors feel they have a good handle on compliance issues, and with additional independent/non-executive directors on the board, they seek ways to work more collaboratively, to yield better options for board decisions. Board members' desire to be more directly involved in fueling transformation propels the board to adopt a different profile.

The Catalyst Board

Catalyst Board: Description and Focus

It would be true to say that most boards place a high value on driving growth (a Foundational Board focus) and good governance (a main goal of Structural Boards) while ensuring the sustainability of the organizations they serve. Yet Catalyst Boards go further by seeing their primary purpose as driving *organizational transformation*. Having gained a handle on compliance and oversight, Catalyst Board directors are interested not only in how they can accelerate value creation for the organizations they serve, but also how they might collaborate and combine their individual talents, networks, and expertise to reinvent how the organization conducts business.

Catalyst Boards often create very different relationships with senior management teams than those formed by Structural Boards. Structural Boards serve as watchdogs and see their role as keeping senior management on the straight and narrow path. Catalyst Boards are more inclined to help senior management teams find ways to innovate, take risks, and experiment – all with an eye toward fueling growth. While the board and senior managers all acknowledge that the board has an important oversight role, all parties work to establish a more collaborative relationship. Senior management teams begin to lean on the board for insight and guidance on potential growth strategies, and they seek board approval for major new initiatives. It is clear to all involved that value creation – whether through the creation of new strategies, the mitigation of risk, or the leveraging of existing opportunities – is the primary goal, with other issues taking a backseat on the board's agenda.

We all know that boards need to have good accountability structures – compliance processes can always be tightened up. But when the large well-publicized failures occur, if we just review structure and not culture, we're missing what's really happening. We need to pay attention to how the board works with management, developing trust, how they support one another – or we're only seeing half of the solution.

– Susan Forrester

Common Traits of the Catalyst Board

The Catalyst Board most often includes a mixture of executive and non-executive directors – with the balance landing in favor of independent directors. Additionally, Catalyst Boards most often have a separate board chairperson and chief executive officer.

Catalyst Boards often operate more like a team than Foundational or Structural Boards. Whereas Foundational Boards value selecting directors from a small group of insiders, Catalyst Boards are more interested in augmenting their team with diverse players who bring skillsets and perspectives that the board does not currently have. This is particularly true when boards are in the process of transformation after a crisis – inviting new players onto the board is seen as a strategy to win back public trust and drive change. This focus often leads the board to grow and become more diverse as new, independent directors bring unique skillsets, networks, and expertise to the board team. For Catalyst Boards, diversity might be seen as a potential driver of growth and therefore a strategic advantage.

Catalyst Boards embrace transformation as a necessary step in organizational development and seek to implement a mind-set of continuous improvement throughout the organization. It's not uncommon for boards that have recently adopted the Catalyst Board profile to make changes in executive leadership – particularly if the organization is coming through a crisis – in the hopes that new leaders will help accelerate the organizational transformation process.

Catalyst Board Meetings and Processes

As Catalyst Boards view themselves more as a team, the way they approach board meetings and other governance work might look quite different than it does in the Foundational or Compliance profiles. Board interactions often become more frequent, and the focus is mostly on discussion. Catalyst Boards are less interested in lengthy reports with detailed data and much more interested in having the senior management team provide analysis, suggested approaches, potential insights, and then share the data to back up their assertions. Meanwhile, directors see their role as one of nudging the senior management team to double-down on potential high-growth strategies and shift resources away from strategies that are less likely to fuel growth.

Catalyst Boards also become more focused on increasing the amount of board education taking place. For example, they might create ad hoc committees to conduct research, work through specific issues, and make recommendations to the board for strategic investments. Catalyst Boards might ask for more background information on issues, including briefings by department heads as well as articles, videos, and other educational materials from outside the organization. Board education might comprise at least a portion of every board meeting, with the goal of helping the Catalyst Board find inspiration on new potential avenues for growth.

Tech and Tools in Use by Catalyst Boards

Catalyst Boards begin to see technology and online tools as essential to help the board perform at a high level. Directors of Catalyst Boards value having secure channels they can use to contact one another before, during, and after meetings. They seek tools that can help them conduct their own research, to review past decisions and results, and to identify potential opportunities and risks. The focus is on finding better ways to facilitate collaboration and building board prowess – such as board peer evaluations, secure messaging, and online board education tools.

Outcomes for Catalyst Boards

Catalyst Boards acknowledge their role in driving organizational growth, and because of this, they are hungry for better data, analyses, insights, and education. While the chief executive takes responsibility for the company's strategy, the board accepts the responsibility for ensuring the chief executive's success – and they hold themselves accountable to ensuring organizational success.

As a result, chief executives have a different relationship with Catalyst Boards as compared to their relationships with Foundational or Structural Boards. With Catalyst Boards, the chief executive and senior management team begin to rely on the board to provide unique perspective and insight, and they begin to involve the board earlier in the process of forming strategies. Because of their focus on growth, Catalyst Boards often lead organizations that outpace their competitors, particularly those organizations with Foundational or Structural Boards.

Catalyst Boards' Key Drivers to Change

As directors become more adept at combining their talents and networks to help their organizations grow, they are more likely to court risk. Sometimes, these risks pay off in rapid, exponential value creation; sometimes, these strategies provide short-term gains while creating longer-term challenges. As directors have a wider range of experiences in serving as catalysts, they often become more circumspect. Partly in response to investor pressure, and partly driven from within, they begin to crave more holistic strategies and sustainable results. They seek out approaches that account for more than just revenue creation and include consideration of environmental, social, and governance factors. At this point, Catalyst Boards might have a slightly reduced appetite for pure experimentation, opting instead for more conservative approaches that offer more nuance.

Meanwhile, as Catalyst Boards become more directly engaged with the organization, they sometimes run the risk of overstepping the boundaries of governance and straying too far into management's territory. If the Catalyst Board's involvement and intervention aren't managed well, they can seem a bit scattershot, constrained both by directors' availability and by management's level of openness to the board's direct engagement across the enterprise. Catalyst Boards that navigate this delicate balance well can experience positive returns – both in terms of company performance and in terms of strengthening a culture of mutual trust and transparency between the board and management. But it definitely poses a risk and can eventually lead Catalyst Boards to desire a different approach.

Most important, the directors of Catalyst Boards begin to desire to have deeper strategic relationships – with the senior management team, with peers in analogous industries, and with shareholders and investors. They begin to see the potential for long-term growth and sustainability through establishing open and ongoing dialog among these groups – with the board serving in a stewardship role as facilitator, instigator, and mediator. These trends propel boards to move away from a turnaround mind-set to a more balanced focus on creating long-term strategic value.

On a start-up board I'm on, they use the board like an extension of the executive team. They try to engage the board in every strategic conversation. At the founding stage, the board might be very engaged – but there are few or no committees, no documentation, no tech tools like board portals. In a public company, by contrast, it might be an incredibly effective board that's been together for a long time with extraordinary executives who try to benchmark themselves in every way. It's considered a well-oiled machine.[8]

– Laurie Yoler

The Futuristic Board

The Futuristic Board: Description and Focus

The Futuristic Board sees itself as the custodian of the organization they serve. They have an eye toward their own legacy and place as high a value on the organization's sustainability as on fueling growth. This does not mean

Futuristic Boards are opposed to innovation – quite the opposite. These directors spur innovation by creating strong networks of support, making strategic investments, and providing insight and foresight to the management team. They see value in adopting sound, ethical governance practices as a strategy to ensure the organization's long-term success.

Directors of Futuristic Boards believe in building strong strategic relationships across their organizations, within their community of investors, across industries, and even within circles of regulatory and legislative influence. Their goal is to put strong bridges in place that can serve as a bulwark against challenges the organization might face, simultaneously working to build trust and goodwill by adopting sound ethical governance practices. These directors drive the governance process in their organizations, continuously challenging themselves to make better-informed, more insightful decisions. Futuristic Boards see themselves as ongoing students of their businesses, building something to withstand the tests of time, with an eye toward ensuring the organization will have a net positive impact on society, the environment, and on governance practices in general.

Futuristic Boards, with their sights set on legacy, trust each other to be accountable. It's not uncommon for Futuristic Board directors to police themselves, even volunteering to step off the board if they believe their skills, expertise, and networks are no longer aligned with where the organization needs to go.

Common Traits of Futuristic Boards

For this board profile, most – if not all – directors are independent, non-executives. It's most common for Futuristic Boards to have a separate board chairperson and chief executive officer. It's also common for these boards to have adopted a specific board-composition policy that values diversity – particularly as directors with unique perspectives and connections can help augment the Futuristic Board's goal of establishing multiple strategic relationships across networks.

Directors of Futuristic Boards often position themselves as coaches to the senior management team. They want to help the executive team succeed – but they don't often feel the need to be directly involved in developing the plans. Rather, they want to help inform executives' plans by bringing a broader perspective, providing keen insight derived from relevant experience, and by leveraging the networks they've established.

Meanwhile, the senior management teams working with Futuristic Boards view their directors as strategic assets. They have deep respect for the knowledge, expertise, and access to networks these directors provide them. Futuristic Boards are likely to find senior management teams eager to bring new ideas for discussion to the board at an early stage because the team trusts the board to provide valuable insight without straying out of the governance "swim lane."

Current governance is more or less based on historical data, and our current frameworks are "backwards-looking" in a time when we need them to be more forward-thinking. Boards need to know what they don't know, which requires a lot of courage. Directors need to be able to ask questions and be honest about what they don't understand, or they won't be able to provide the level of oversight and insight required today.[9]

– Dr. Anastassia Lauterbach

Futuristic Board Meetings and Processes

Futuristic Board meetings vary in length – some lasting only a couple of hours, others lasting much longer – with an agenda chock-full of strategic discussion. Directors drive the agenda for these meetings. They often will task themselves with conducting their own research in preparation for a discussion, reaching out to the management team for clarification and additional data as needed.

Futuristic Board directors see it as their job to engage with their organizations at multiple levels. One might find Futuristic Board directors attending select senior management team meetings as "silent observers," with the goal of quietly absorbing the nuances of the team's discussion to help inform decisions the board might make in the future.

Futuristic Boards also make strategic use of committees. As in other stages, Futuristic Board committees are relied upon to work through details and make recommendations back to the full board. But beyond this, Futuristic Boards might leverage committees as a pipeline for future talent by inviting the outside participation of non–board members or of rising stars within the organization's staff.

Tech and Tools in Use by Futuristic Boards

For this board profile, directors feel a need to have robust tools to help organize, secure, and facilitate the governance role. Futuristic Boards might adopt technology systems that serve up custom content and insights for directors; provide opportunities for data visualization; facilitate peer networking; or offer high-level "scorecards" on areas of compliance, risk, and overall board effectiveness. Futuristic Board directors demand innovative tools that can keep up with how they want to perform the governance role. It's not uncommon for these boards to establish strategic relationships with technology vendors, particularly if the vendor is open to engaging with Futuristic Board directors on possible future innovations for their offerings.

Outcomes for Futuristic Boards

Futuristic Boards understand their role is to serve as a strategic asset for their organizations. The organization's destiny is seen to be tied to the success of the board to serve as prudent stewards of the mission while simultaneously propelling the organization to innovate. Directors adopt the role of "coaches in chief," helping their chief executives become strong and capable leaders.

As a result, it's not uncommon to see articles written about Futuristic Boards. They are usually associated with some of the most successful organizations – those that have maintained growth over long periods of time, have demonstrated futuristic tendencies in the face of challenges, and have had a string of capable leaders at the helm.

Take a look at a company like IKEA, which was smart enough to buy TaskRabbit, a new gig economy marketplace for connecting people who wanted tasks done. That's the kind of thinking you get from a "futurist-minded" board, one that really understands how technology is going to change the business, one that recognized that retail is now all "experiential," and you can't expect retail businesses to work as they did years ago at Sears or Circuit City – two formerly successful, and now dead, companies. The old model of retail is a "cadaver" on the side of the road.[10]

– Betsy Atkins

Futuristic Boards' Key Drivers to Change

Given the Futuristic Board's focus on their long-term "legacy," it's not uncommon for directors to self-identify when it's time for them to step aside and make room for fresh perspectives. Indeed, many Futuristic Boards view leadership succession planning as one of their most important roles – even holding themselves accountable to ensure there are succession plans in place for top executives as well as directors.

For many Futuristic Boards, turnover does not prove overly disrupting – particularly when there are only a small number of changes to the membership in a given period of time. However, should there be rapid or widescale turnover of board membership – for example, in the case of a major organizational transformation, as might happen in a merger or acquisition – the board could rapidly change its profile as new directors come on board and work to find their footing.

Notes

1. In the United States, many family businesses do not form a board of directors until they reach a certain size or change their corporate structure. A good summary of the complexities of U.S. family enterprise boards was written in 2001 by John Davis for Harvard

Business Working Knowledge, entitled "Organizing the Family-Run Business," https://hbswk.hbs.edu/item /organizing-the-family-run-business.

2. Excerpt from telephone interview with Colin Low, 14 Aug. 2018.

3. For nonprofit organizations, this might not be true. However, for nonprofits with this board profile, it's not uncommon for executives to play an active role at board meetings – creating the board's agenda, bringing issues for a vote, and weighing in during board discussions.

4. Excerpt from telephone interview with Jan Babiak, 16 Aug. 2018.

5. David F. Larcker and Brian Tayan, *Corporate Governance Matters: A Closer Look at Organizational Choices and Their Consequences* (Old Tappan, NJ: Pearson Education, 2016).

6. Over the past 10 years, many countries in the European Union have increased their requirements around director independence, with the majority of countries now requiring at least one-third of directors to be completely independent from the organization. Subodh Mishra and Institutional Shareholder Services, Inc., "Global Governance: Board Independence Standards and Practices," Grading Global Boards of Directors on Cybersecurity, https:// corpgov.law.harvard.edu/2018/06/01/global-governance -board-independence-standards-and-practices/.

7. Excerpt from telephone interview with Nora Denzel, 6 Sept. 2018.

8. Excerpt from telephone interview with Laurie Yoler, 2 Aug. 2018.

9. Excerpt from telephone interview with Anastassia Lauterbach, PhD, 15 Aug. 2018.

10. Excerpt from telephone interview with Betsy Atkins, 21 Aug. 2018.

CHAPTER 8

Board Behavioral Profiles in Action

How Boards of Each Profile Approach Best Practice

A construction company's board brings in a director from the retail world. The board of a global engine manufacturer radically overhauls its director-management communications. Site visits become the norm, and tech and cyber issues find a regular place on the meeting agenda. Around the world, governance professionals are evolving business as usual for the digital age, exhibiting traits of specific Board Behavioral Profiles and shifting profiles when necessary – consciously or unconsciously.

How can your board use the Board Behavioral Profiles to boost its performance in value creation; resilience; risk management; strategy; environmental, sustainability, and governance ESG issues; and personal accountability? Knowledge is half the battle. The sections below show representative tendencies for each profile in each area.

Where does your board currently fall? Where might it need to shift, for right now and in the future?

Value Creation

- **Foundational Board.** Growth-focused, but often as an extension of management team, with limited governance resources, and experience.
- **Structural Board.** Asks questions and uses online tools, but its "caretaker approach" and strict oversight focus may stifle value creation.
- **Catalyst Board.** Supported by innovation committees, multiperspective conversations, and ongoing director education, prioritizes value creation with a "private equity" approach that may hinder risk management.
- **Futuristic Board.** To provide foresight and insight to management team, focuses on strong networks, strategic investments, and sound ethical governance practices.

Resilience

- **Foundational Board.** Often a small group of insiders, a lack of diverse perspectives may make it vulnerable to unexpected shifts in the marketplace.
- **Structural Board.** Strong in legal/compliance expertise, oversight focus fuels the push for processes, tools, and more independent directors for checks and balances.
- **Catalyst Board.** Directors with diverse perspectives and skillsets and results orientation, seeking evaluations that go beyond "checking the box," more frequent, candid conversations supported by research and tools.
- **Futuristic Board.** Diversity both a priority and a policy, with directors expanding talent pipelines, employing skills matrices, actively engaging in networking and self-education.

Risk Management

- **Foundational Board.** Reactively takes direction from management with limited tools, documentation, and governance experience.
- **Structural Board.** Takes strong oversight focus (sometimes overshadowing other priorities), with detailed meeting agendas and crisis-response plans.
- **Catalyst Board.** More likely to court risk in the quest for growth, yet diverse board perspectives, including those of CIO/CISO directors, and use of third-party data and tools may act as a safeguard.
- **Futuristic Board.** Uses strong strategic relationships (with investors, industry, regulators) as a bulwark against challenges.

Strategy/Just-in-Time Insight

- **Foundational Board.** May be very engaged (particularly if a start-up), but may have few processes or structures and may not yet recognize their potentially powerful role as strategic advisor.
- **Structural Board.** More accustomed to asking questions (though often those of a "watchdog" focus) and often looks to management for answers.
- **Catalyst Board.** Acting as a counselor, guides growth strategies (often outpacing competitors), partners with management and stakeholders, and seeks insight from peers to innovate, take risks, and experiment.
- **Futuristic Board.** As coach and advisor, drives the strategic agenda with a focus on innovation and sustainability and an in-depth understanding of how technology is changing their business.

ESG

- **Foundational Board.** Directors consider ESG issues as they relate to growth, efficiency, and making an impact.
- **Structural Board.** Regulatory/reporting requirements drive ESG activities, including use of compliance and "audit trail" tools.
- **Catalyst Board.** Diverse boards elevate ESG issues beyond revenue and compliance and integrate them more holistically into strategy, tracking issues, educating directors, and conducting ongoing dialogues with employees and stakeholders.
- **Futuristic Board.** Directors consider ESG issues in context of legacy, focused on making an overall positive impact on society, the environment, and governance.

Personal Accountability

- **Foundational Board.** Directors often have "skin in the game," but limited tools and resources for growing as governance professionals or challenging management.
- **Structural Board.** Supported by more policies, structures, and tools, directors recognize their role as "questioners in chief," especially after a major legal/ethical crisis, and may seek better analyses and more collaboration.
- **Catalyst Board.** Directors operate as a team, actively seeking their own data sources, analyses, and relationships both within and outside of the company.
- **Futuristic Board.** Legacy-focused directors prioritize a culture of trust, candor, and accountability, and recognize the need for board refreshment, including when it's time to step aside themselves.

In Conclusion ...

Governance is in the midst of transformation, and we have yet to see how the story will end. In the preceding chapters, we've attempted to collect, summarize, augment, and share insights from directors and executives, researchers, reporters, and others as a way to expand the global conversation on governance best practices. But what amounts to "best practices" continues to evolve as rapidly as new technologies evolve, and what works well today might outright fail in another time and context.

What matters most in this era defined by volatility, uncertainty, complexity, and ambiguity is building *resilience*. For directors, this means continuously challenging themselves to learn and adapt, and to not be easily satisfied with the status quo. For organizations, it means cultivating a board culture that values adaptability in governing, actively seeking out and incorporating diverse perspectives and voices in order to gain the most expansive vantage point on board decisions.

Directors who place a high value on their own curiosity – and relentlessly seek to satisfy that curiosity – will be in the best position to lead the most successful enterprises. Those who have little direct technology expertise should be the most hungry, the most eager to gain knowledge – and should be the most welcoming of bringing additional technology experts into the boardroom. In the digital age, the "winners" will be those directors who are perennial "students of the business" – who remain hungry for insight, and don't rest their decisions on well-worn assumptions.

That said, we know that this book has only scratched the surface of all there is to learn about governing successfully in the digital age, and that there will be much more to say in the coming months and years. We hope you'll be inspired to engage in the conversation and connect with us at https://diligent.com/governance -in-the-digital-age. Like the many directors and executives who contributed their insights to this book, we hope you will be inspired to share your stories and participate in creating guidance to inform future peers.

Index

Note: Page references in *italics* refer to figures.